The Moral Majority: Right or Wrong?

The Moral Majority: Right or Wrong?

Robert E. Webber

CROSSWAY BOOKS • WESTCHESTER, ILLINOIS
A DIVISION OF GOOD NEWS PUBLISHERS

Dedicated to my children:

John
Alexandra
Stefany
Jeremy

Contents

Acknowledgments

There are a number of people who have played a vital part in the formation of this book. I wish first to thank my wife, Joanne, for suggesting I write this book and Carl Horn, Peter Means, and Patrick Miller for helping me sort through a number of ideas at the early stage of gathering materials.

I especially appreciate the critical reviews of the first draft and suggestions for improvement made by Cal Thomas, Arthur Holmes, and Harold Lindsell, and the input of Martin E. Marty made by phone consultation. A special word of thanks is due to Charlie Pinches, a graduate student in social ethics at Notre Dame, for his careful reading of the original manuscript and thoughtful suggestions for sharpening the focus of the Christocentric nature of the church. The editorial insights of both Isabel Erickson and Jan Dennis were most helpful in improving the organization and style of the book. And finally, I want to thank Amy Richards for her skillful typing and re-typing of the manuscript.

Chapter One

Introduction

If you were born in or before 1960 you have lived through one of the most tumultuous times of American history. The sixties unleashed two sweeping revolutions, the civil rights and antiwar movements, spearheaded by the youth of this country and heavily supported by the mainline churches. Even now the images burn in our minds and hearts: Martin Luther King, sweat pouring down his face as he preached peace and justice; heads smashed by police billy clubs at the 1968 Democratic Convention; a vast ocean of bodies surging into Washington for the Vietnam Moratorium; John Kennedy, then Bobby, then Martin Luther King—assassinated; four dead at Kent State. And all of it brought smack-dab into our living rooms by television. An entire generation was never the same again.

Then, almost without warning, these revolutions petered out in the seventies. A radical redirection of interest turned marchers and protesters into what Tom Wolfe has called the "me generation." Meanwhile the world woke up to staggering problems—mass starvation in Biafra, Bangladesh, North Africa; hunger in two-thirds of the world, over-abundance in the other third; revolutions in the Third World; skyrocketing energy costs punctuated by block-long gas lines; wholesale destruction of the environment;

double-digit inflation; religious persecution in communist countries; a powder keg in the Middle East; local and international terrorists like the Baader-Meinhof Gang, the Irish Republican Army, Italy's Red Guard; skyjacking; and the menace of nuclear war.

America showed signs of collapse. Urban violent crimes doubled; the divorce rate reached fifty percent; abortion was made available to anyone who wanted it; porno shops and massage parlors sprang up like ragweed; population control groups distributed contraceptives to teens.

Simultaneously, "liberationists" began to demand their rights. Homosexuals and lesbians sought gay rights; feminists lobbied for the Equal Rights Amendment; blacks agitated for education and jobs; Hispanics, Native Americans, Orientals demanded their fair share; the poor and needy reached out for help; ban the bomb and no nuke movements began to call for disarmament; Green peace, Friends of the Earth, the Sierra Club, Project Jonah, and others worked to save the environment.

But the seventies have faded into a new era. Ronald Reagan is in, Jimmy Carter is out. Jerry Falwell has replaced Jerry Rubin in the media spotlight. Phyllis Schlafly is hot, Bella Abzug is not. A backlash against big government, moral decadence, military weakness, and soft political leadership is sweeping the country. There is a movement afoot to "get this country working again," a desire to "bring America back to its moral and religious greatness."

How has the church fared in the midst of these revolutionary changes? That is what this book sets out to investigate. It is about the church on the left—the church in support of liberation movements aimed at breaking the shackles that keep humanity from growing toward its fulfillment; it is also about the church on the right—the church that was silent during these revolutions but has now emerged with a sudden burst of leadership to carry this nation back to faith and morality.

But this book is also about the church that is not completely comfortable with the approach of the church on the
left or the church on the right. This "third way" takes
definite exception to the theological ideology and methodology of the Moral Majority and the World Council of
Churches. It is the church of the prophetic center.★

Before it is possible to set forth the viewpoint of the
prophetic center or to offer its critique of the Moral Majority or the WCC, it is necessary to state its understanding of
the church in the world.

Centrists identify two essential distinctions about the nature of the church and its role in the world: the church is
both a *divine institution* and *the people of God.*

First, the church is a *divine institution* which takes shape
both as local congregations and the larger worldwide community of communities. The local church is the gathering
of Christians in a particular geographical area governed by
a recognized ministry; gathered for worship, teaching, and
fellowship; united in a concern for evangelism and service
in the community. The church as a community of communities is the universal church divided into a number of
subcommunities (e.g., Catholic, Orthodox, Protestant,
Fundamental, Evangelical, Charismatic). These communities are united by faith in Christ, an ordained ministry,
scripture and creeds, worship, the sacraments, and a responsible life in the world. The point to keep in mind about
the church as a divine institution is the principle that *it
should seek no earthly political power because it belongs to the
Kingdom which is not of this world (John 17:14) and has no
affinity with the powers which rule this world (Eph. 2:2).*

Second, the church is *the people of God,* made up of individual Christians who belong to a worldwide society of

---

★I frequently use the word *centrist* to describe this group as well. The full
meaning of the terms *prophetic center* and *centrists* will gradually become
apparent. In chapters 8-13 I deal with this group at length and show their
relationship to a broad evangelicalism.

believers who are united together by their faith in Jesus
Christ as Lord, willing to give him their ultimate allegiance, and seeking to live in an obedience to his commands. These convictions arise from their commitment to
Jesus Christ and the working out of his ethic in the church,
his body. Nevertheless, these believers live out their lives
amid the fallen powers of this world where they are called
to be radically obedient to Christ as Lord in all areas of their
life and work. Thus, the second principle about the church
in the world is that *the church as the people of God is in constant
confrontation and engagement with the fallen powers which control all levels of the social order (Eph. 6:12).*

An inadequate understanding of this dual character of the
church leads to the confusion and compromise which characterize the social agenda of both the Moral Majority and
the World Council of Churches.

This book is a critique of the Moral Majority and the
WCC from this perspective. More importantly, it sets
forth the biblical foundations for the prophetic center as a
witness to society and invites the Moral Majority and the
WCC to forsake the compromise they make with the fallen
powers of this world and to act in greater accord with the
scriptures.

To begin, I will briefly summarize the major features of
the right and the left and sketch out the distinctives of the
prophetic center.

On the Right: The Moral Majority

A brief survey of Jerry Falwell's book *Listen America*,[1]
which represents the agenda of the Moral Majority, shows
that his movement is aligned with many concerns of the
American right.

Falwell believes America has been chosen by God for a
special mission to the world. He views the events of the
twentieth century as having had a negative effect on America's "calling" and demands a repudiation of the secular

forces which are eating away the foundations of this country.

Falwell's thesis is that both godless communism and secular humanism have infiltrated society and will eventually, unless stopped by a return to moral principles, destroy this nation and its mission to the world.

Falwell wants to make America great again. He believes the answer is a return to the free enterprise system, positive patriotism, the religion of the founding fathers, and strong military defense.

Some of the stands which will "help turn this nation around again" include defeat of the Equal Rights Amendment, a constitutional amendment against abortion, and laws prohibiting such sexual permissiveness as smut peddling, contraceptives for teens, and gay rights. He is equally concerned about the loose morality that has permeated movies, television, literature, music, and is available on news stands everywhere. Our society, he believes, is bombarded by moral decline, the breakdown of the family, and the lowering of standards in every area of life.

Furthermore, he is against big government and its increasing encroachment in the family, education, business, the church. He wants to reduce federal spending, lower the taxes, increase military spending, and restore American dignity around the world.

The main arguments of the religious right may be set forth in four major propositions. They are:

1. Biblical morality and freedom are central to God's plan for people and nations.
2. The free enterprise system and the political structure of capitalism are mandated by scripture and therefore related to biblical morality.
3. America is a country chosen by God to be an example of a nation built on the biblical teaching of a free enterprise system and Christian morality. Its role in the world is to preach the gospel and spread the values of freedom and morality.

4. The church and other moral people must-rise up to save America by returning it to its original economic, political, and spiritual principles.*

On the Left: The World Council of Churches

A brief survey of the reports from the World Council of Churches in Nairobi in 1975 shows that mainline church leadership aligns itself with issues on the left.[2]

The leaders of the church on the left express their concern for the peoples of the world who are oppressed by economic exploitation, discrimination, and the perpetuation of injustices. They clearly charge American capitalism and the imperialistic policies of this "oppressive and godless nation" as the major cause for these problems.

Consequently, they opt for socialism (some for communism) as the answer to the economic problems of the world and call for a revolution to free the poor from their oppressors. They freely use the Marxist critique of capitalist society and see the destruction of capitalism as part of the liberating process necessary to establish justice for the poor, the oppressed, and those who are discriminated against on the basis of sex, color, or race.

The gospel is understood in terms of liberation: as God through Moses liberated the people of Israel from their oppressor, so today the church must join forces with those movements which intend to liberate people from economic, political, and social oppression. This is a process which takes place in history through the action of God. God the great liberator is exemplified in Jesus Christ who frees us from sin. Since sin is manifested in the imperfection of society, the gospel of liberation must occur within the social history of the world.

Consequently, the left calls on the church to join hands

*It must be recognized that not all believers or local congregations who support the Moral Majority understand its ideological basis.

with the revolutions of the world to free the oppressed and needy. For this reason, the left supports government welfare programs, the Equal Rights Amendment, government legislation to grant equal rights for homosexuals, and government support of blacks and other minority groups. The left is equally concerned to hold back government spending for military purposes, argues for disarmament, and supports legislation for the preservation of the environment.

In brief, the major concerns of the left, which seem diametrically opposed to those on the right, may be summarized in the following four statements.

1. Justice and concern for the poor is central to the biblical vision of life.
2. The Marxist critique of capitalism as the major source of injustice is correct. Therefore, the overthrow of capitalism (sometimes through violence) is desirable as a means through which socialism (which is more true to biblical teaching) may be established.
3. America is an imperialistic nation which supports right-wing governments, uses an unfair amount of the world's resources, and is indifferent to the needs of the poor and the oppressed.
4. The church must take sides against the oppressor (capitalism) in support of all economic, political, and personal liberation movements.*

The Prophetic Center
Although the Moral Majority and the World Council of Churches represent the viewpoint of many Christians who are socially active, these two approaches are not the only alternatives. There is a third way which is more consistent with scripture and orthodoxy—the prophetic center. I shall mention some of the characteristics of the centrist view-

---

*It must be recognized that many believers and local congregations who are associated with the WCC do not support their agenda or point of view.

point which will be developed more fully later in the book.

First, the prophetic center finds its ultimate point of reference in Jesus Christ. It regards the Old Testament as subject to progressive revelation, which is fulfilled in Jesus Christ, the fullness of God's revelation. Because God was made flesh in Jesus Christ, an understanding of who Jesus was, what his work accomplished in terms of the Kingdom, and what his example means for Christian living is the final authority in matters of social responsibility.

Second, the centrist regards the church as the extension of Christ's presence in time and space. The church is, therefore, the focus of God's activity in the world. God has revealed himself to the church through Jesus Christ, and he is working in and through the church to manifest his victory over sin, death, and the dominion of the devil. Thus the church is a unique "society within the society" which calls people into a relationship with Jesus Christ and mediates his values to the fallen world.

Third, the prophetic center rejects a rigid privatistic moralism on the one hand and an exclusivistic religion of the poor on the other hand. This does not mean that centrists are against morality or have no concern for the poor. On the contrary, centrists seek to build a case for morality and concern for the poor on the basis of a biblical world view. This viewpoint frees centrists from the choice of private ethics on the one hand and public ethics on the other. It insists, instead, that there is only one ethic given to the church which must be lived out in one's private life and in one's activity in the world.

For these reasons the prophetic center takes issue with both the right and the left in several areas.

First, centrists reject the notion that there is a particular economic or political system that is sanctioned by biblical teaching. Rather, centrists argue that all structures of society (except the church) are under the "powers" and controlled by the dominion of evil. Because people are fallen sinful human beings, they can misuse any economic or political system and through it express the evil intent of their hearts. In this, centrists reject allegiance either to capitalist or socialist systems as *the* system God supports!

Second, centrists reject the notion that America or any other nation has been chosen by God to be God's special people. In a fallen world there can be no such thing as a "Christian nation." America is not now, nor has it ever been a Christian nation. The best that can be said for this country is that the influence of Christian values have exercised a restraining influence on sin—a restraint which has surely waned considerably in the last few decades.

Third, centrists reject the leftist notion that God is working through the revolutions of history to bring about his Kingdom. This notion is a perversion of the gospel which results in the sanctioning of violent revolution. And it, like the notion that America is a special nation, is a utopianism that replaces the Christian hope in the consummation with the mistaken notion that the Kingdom can be achieved on earth apart from the direct intervention of God.

Fourth, since the centrist sees the focus of God's work in the church, his supernatural people on earth, the centrist calls for the church to find ways to mediate its values to the fallen social order.

These are issues which go to the very heart of social ethics. Centrists insist on a biblically radical ethic which refuses to confuse the place and role of the church with the place and role of the state or other societal institutions. Centrists refuse to have a double ethic—one for the private life and another for public vocation. There is only one ethic which is given to the divine institution of the church, and the people of God who belong to the church are called to live and act out this ethic in the context of a pagan world.

Conclusion
Let it be clear that the position espoused in this book is not

a compromise between the left and the right, but a sharp
and distinct alternative. It is based on a radical understanding of evil—that mankind's rebellion against God has
affected all of humanity in history. It is based on a radical
understanding of Jesus Christ—that he is the God-Man
who by his death and resurrection destroyed the power of
evil and the dominion of the devil in this world (a work to
be completed at the second coming of Christ). It is based on
a radical understanding of the church—that the church is
the "body" of Christ, the community of his presence in the
world, the presence of the Kingdom, and that Christians
give their ultimate allegiance to Jesus Christ as Lord. Consequently, the church cannot compromise its loyalty to
Christ by making any "holy alliances" with the fallen powers. In this context both the Moral Majority and the World
Council of Churches stand under the judgment of biblical
revelation.

Part I

Turn to the Right:
The Moral Majority

Chapter Two

Capitalism

It is generally accepted that this country has taken a turn to the right. The mandate given to Ronald Reagan in 1980 was not only a rejection of the more liberal policies of the Carter administration, but a cry for leadership of a different sort.

The irony is that in 1976 many evangelicals and fundamentalists supported Jimmy Carter's promise of a "different kind of leadership." Fundamentalists perceived a definite lack of Christian conviction in Carter's leadership, however, which led them and many evangelicals to support the Moral Majority and the so-called new right. Why? This question must be answered against the background of fundamentalism in America.

Fundamentalist Background
It is generally recognized by historians and theologians that the origins of Protestant social concern in this country are found in nineteenth-century revivalism. However, in the early decades of the twentieth century a split occurred between the churches dividing them into fundamentalist and modernist camps. As the modernists began to preach their social gospel, the fundamentalists saw themselves as the protectors of orthodox theology.

The popular conception of the fundamentalist minority of this time was underscored by the famous Scopes Trial of 1925. In this trial Clarence Darrow made fundamentalists appear as intolerant bigots and anti-intellectual fools. Unfortunately, the rise of higher criticism, the optimistic view of man, and the more naturalistic view of the Christian faith which were all accepted among the so-called "religious intellectuals" of that time put the fundamentalists into a most unfortunate and ill light. They became the despised minority, the backwoods preachers, the unenlightened ones.

After World War II a group of fundamentalists associated with Billy Graham demanded a restoration of social concern. These leaders and those who associated with them became known as neo-evangelicals.

Between 1947 and 1976 the fundamentalists avoided social issues and accused the neo-evangelicals of being soft on modernism. Consequently, these two groups have been unfriendly toward each other, even though the lines are not absolutely drawn between them.

How did fundamentalism, which was so opposed to the social gospel, become involved in social issues? Two current events spurred the fundamentalists into action. The first was the bicentennial. Fundamentalism experienced a tremendous upsurge of patriotism as a result of the anti-Americanism of the sixties. The bicentennial gave fundamentalists the opportunity to express their positive feelings about America through the "I Love America" programs held in Washington, D.C. and many other cities in America. In these meetings the fundamentalists focused on the role of religion in the founding of America, the religious commitment of America's fathers, and the idea of America's special place as a "Christian nation" in the world.

The fundamentalist emphasis on America's heritage was coupled with the accusation that the religious emphasis in

America had been lost and replaced by a secular humanism. These "new patriots" drew the battle line for the future of America between their camp which argued for a restoration of American principles and the secular humanists who were bringing about the downfall of this nation.

Secondly, certain actions on the part of the "godless secularists" unleashed the potential of this movement. These were the questioning of the tax exempt status of religious schools and organizations by the IRS; the newly formed federal abortion laws; the inability to define obscenity and pornography resulting in the subsequent rise of indecency in movies and TV; the emergence of the feminists in the equal rights movement; the gay rights movement; the loss of America's military supremacy and subsequent vulnerability to communism; the rapid rise of divorce resulting in the breakdown of the family; the rising crime rate; double digit inflation; and the failure of Jimmy Carter to deliver Christian leadership. The slumbering giant of fundamentalism had been awakened—and most appropriately it called itself the Moral Majority!

The Ideological Basis
The manifesto of the Moral Majority, set forth in Jerry Falwell's book *Listen America,* consists of two basic premises: the straightforward use of the Bible, and the assertion that the Bible teaches the free enterprise system. These are the two sources from which his ideology and that of Moral Majority derive.

The Straightforward Use of the Bible
The biblical theme which is the foundation for Falwell's patriotic and religious conviction is a passage from Proverbs 14:34: "Righteousness exalteth a nation; but sin is a reproach to any people." "It is right living that has made America the greatest nation on earth," says Falwell, "and with all of her shortcomings and failures, America is with-

out question the greatest nation on the face of God's earth."[1] However, his burden is that America will lose her privileged place in God's world because of a failure of godly leadership on the one hand and the moral decadence of her people on the other. These two themes are developed in several ways.

First, Falwell points to the biblical teaching that rulers are ordained of God (see Romans 13). This passage, he writes, "does not imply that all persons in places of authority are godly people. It does, however, mean that they are in their positions whether they are aware of the fact or not, by divine ordination."[2] Rulers can be either ministers of terror or good; therefore, Americans "have a grave responsibility to vote in those leaders who will rule America justly, under divine guidance."[3]

Second, the Bible admonishes people to pray for their rulers. Falwell quotes I Timothy 2:1-3 and calls for Christians to "pray for those in authority." This passage is also a reminder to the leaders of this country that America's future is in their hands and that they will one day "stand before God accountable with what they have done to ensure our future." America, he says, "needs men and women of God who have an understanding of the times and are not afraid to stand up for what is right."[4]

Falwell's third concern is that there has been a failure of godly and moral leadership in America. This is the reason why there is so much "confusion and selfishness, which is destroying the very basis of our society," he says. For this reason he insists that "when society begins to fall apart spiritually, what we find missing is the mighty man—that man who is willing, with courage and confidence, to stand up for what is right."[5]

Because there is no "mighty man" to lead America, Americans are making a god of government by seeking their security in it. Americans are "looking to government rather than to God, who ordained government," says Falwell.[6]

What is Falwell's solution to this spiritual decay, moral corruption, and deification of government?

He believes Americans must return to the biblical basis on which this country was founded. "God promoted America to a greatness no other nation has ever enjoyed," says Falwell, "because her heritage is one of a republic governed by laws predicated on the Bible." For that reason we must return to the biblical basis on which this nation was founded. Falwell is optimistic that America can be turned around because "there is still a vast number of Americans who love their country, are patriotic, and are willing to sacrifice for her."[7]

The Bible Teaches the Free Enterprise System

Having set forth the premise that the Bible is the basis of this nation, Falwell launches into an application of biblical principles to the issue of economics. He sets forth his case for the interrelationship between politics, economics, and moral decadence by assuming that there is a biblical basis for the free enterprise system and insisting that contemporary conservative economists express a biblical economics. These two ideas lie at the base of the entire Moral Majority agenda.

First, Falwell sets forth his belief that the free enterprise system is biblical in the following statement:

The free enterprise system is clearly outlined in the Book of Proverbs in the Bible. Jesus Christ made it clear that the work ethic was a part of His plan for man. Ownership of property is Biblical. Competition in business is Biblical. Ambitious and successful business management is clearly outlined as a part of God's plan for His people.[8]

Unfortunately, no clear and systematic biblical argument for the above assertion is set forth in *Listen America*. This does not mean, however, that a case for free enterprise or capitalism as biblical has not been made by others, upon whom Falwell may be dependent.

Although he gives no biblical argument for the free enterprise system, Falwell reads the biblical statements on property, the work ethic, and management through the grid of contemporary conservative economists and politicians.

For example, the influence on Falwell's political and economic system can be adduced from the persons quoted and the specialized statements they make to support the basic political and economic commitment of the Moral Majority. The persons on whom the Moral Majority are most dependent are economist Milton Friedman (*Free to Choose*) and the politicians Jesse Helms (*When Free Men Shall Stand*), and William E. Simon (*A Time For Truth*).

Here are several examples of their economic viewpoint which Falwell quotes favorably:

Milton Friedman:

The economic controls that have proliferated in the United States in recent decades have not only restricted our freedom to use our economic resources, they have also affected our freedom of speech, of press, and of religion.[9]

Jesse Helms:

In recent years there has been a rising tide of criticism of "the system." The criticism for the most part, has been neither fair nor valid. The system is excellent; the primary fault lies with politicians and legislators and bureaucrats and judges in high places who have manhandled, not only the system, but the very meaning of freedom itself. As a consequence the future of this country, as long as they are in charge of it, is depressingly bleak.[10]

William Simon:

Our country today sits at the very crossroads between freedom and totalitarian rule. If a majority of Americans do not soon understand this reality and help turn the tide toward freedom, they ultimately will have no choice, but to understand it at a time when it will be too late to do anything about it.[11]

Though *Listen America* is filled with conservative economic and political opinions Falwell is neither an economist nor a politician. He is primarily a preacher with a burden for morality. He wants to help turn this country back to moral principles—both private and public. It so happens that, in his view, morality, economics, and politics are so intertwined in American government that it is impossible to talk of one without the other. Falwell's comments concerning economics and politics must be read in that light.

Nevertheless, there is a question that must be asked: did conservative politicians and economists use Falwell and other TV preachers as a means to propagate their views? A statement made by one of the most avid promoters of the right, Richard Viguerie, the direct mail master fundraiser of New Right Cause, seems to support the fear that Falwell was used by the right. According to the Evangelical Press News Service (November 1, 1980) Viguerie confirmed "the widespread suspicion that highly visible television evangelists were recruited to the cause of conservative politics by a handful of veteran far-right organizers." Besides himself, Viguerie identified Robert J. Billings, one of the founders of Moral Majority; E. E. McAteer, a veteran right-wing lobbyist in Washington and former director of Conservative Caucus (identified by critics as the largest "extremist" right-wing organization); and Howard Phillips, a former aide to Richard Nixon and founder of Conservative Caucus. This seems to suggest that the conservative right which is rooted in an American civil religion has used Falwell as a spokesman for their ideology. Further evidence of Falwell's new right involvement comes from the fact that he wrote the introduction to Richard

Viguerie's book, *The New Right: We're Ready to Lead.*

We may conclude from this discussion that the Moral Majority has an ideology which unites biblical morality with capitalist economics resulting in a "Christian nationalism." It is a mixture of religion and politics.

Criticism

It must be recognized, especially by Christians, that there is a fundamental truth to the concerns of the Moral Majority. It is an incontestable fact that the moral fiber of this country and its citizens has undergone a fundamental change since World War II, and especially since the revolutionary era of the 1960s. During this time we have lost our sense of God's transcendence, and with it, a loss of the values which are connected with the confession that God, not the government, is the final source of human values. Nevertheless, the answer which Jerry Falwell sets forth is marred by several shortcomings.

First, the emphasis on the recovery of morals is rooted in an American moralism which is associated with civil religion.* American civil religion has always advocated basic human morals as necessary to the strength of America and its mission to spread liberty, human dignity, and basic decency. Falwell admits that his aim is to bring together all who support the return to a moral America regardless of their religious commitment. This reduces moral principles to rules or regulations that are not necessarily a part of personal convictions but can exist in an impersonal and objective way. Consequently, it is sufficient to establish "objective laws" by "legislation" to which people conform in an outward manner.

This approach to values has its place, but it is not distinctly Christian, and its error is that it blurs the distinction

---

*Civil religion may be defined as the state's use of religion for its own political ends.

which Christians should make between "outward conformity to moral values" and the "inward conviction born
of regeneration in Jesus Christ followed by obedience to his
teaching and example." For biblical Christianity, morality
in and of itself is not enough. There must be personal regeneration by faith in Jesus Christ and association with his
church because the ultimate source of true values is found
in God's revelation in Jesus Christ transmitted through the
church. A truly Christian approach to morality in government invites those who govern to receive Jesus Christ and
follow his values in radical obedience. The establishment of
morals derives from inner conviction and obedience rather
than a mere outward conformity. Consequently, Falwell's
alternative to the current moral decadence of America is
more consistent with the morality of civil religion than the
morality of the Christian faith. Furthermore, mere moralism, especially when it is advocated by the church, may
result in the church as moral watchdog turning into the
church as moral policeman.

A second criticism of Falwell's ideology is that it is too
optimistic about the nature of humanity. This is evident in
his uncritical support of the free enterprise system. Even if a
good case can be made for free enterprise, the failure to
recognize the misuse and abuse of this system by those who
are motivated by greed is a major flaw. Falwell seems to
assume a basic goodness in the human personality which
the Bible itself rejects. He does not sufficiently recognize
the biblical picture of human selfishness and greed. The
history of capitalism and the free enterprise system shows
how sinful persons motivated by the desire for material
wealth and power have created an imbalance between the
rich and the poor, promoted or allowed discrimination,
abused nature, and contributed to the dehumanization of
the working masses. These results are not due to the system
as much as they are due to the sinfulness of persons within
the system. A proper view of the social order refuses to

sanction any human system as biblical, recognizing that all structures, except the church, are ruled by the "powers" of evil.

A third criticism may be directed toward the "mighty man" theory which Falwell advocates. This notion of a mighty man raised up to lead the nation back to morality is extremely dangerous. It smacks of Nietzsche's superman—Hitler's model for himself—or Jim Jones, or Sun Myung Moon. It is particularly frightful when the mighty man forces his viewpoint on the populace through legislation, manipulation of the emotions, or coercion. The government then becomes a tool of political religion, which, because of its power and sway, controls the minds and actions of all but the strongest members of society. This is exactly what happened in Germany.

The biblical vision of the mighty man is Jesus Christ who in his death and resurrection was victor over sin, death, and the dominion of the devil. The Christian church owes him ultimate allegiance, is shaped by his self-sacrificing example, and awaits his consummation for the final overthrow of sin and the establishment of his Kingdom. Thus, the church as a divine institution is a distinct "society within the society" which does not seek to establish the Kingdom on earth through an allegiance with the power structure of any particular national government or the charisma of any national Christian leader.

Chapter Three

A Chosen Nation

The Moral Majority says America is a Christian nation called by God to fulfill a special mission to the world. Is this true? In this chapter we will first examine the evidence for this claim, then critique it.

The Christian Foundations of America

In *Listen America* Falwell sets forth four arguments in support of the notion that America was founded as a nation with a strong Christian influence.

First, America was "founded by godly men upon godly principles to be a Christian nation."[1] This does not mean that all the founding fathers were Christians. Nevertheless, they were guided by biblical principles and earnestly sought to develop a nation which would reflect these ideals.

For example, the original vision of a nation "under God" was set forth by the Puritans who "had come in search of a place where they could freely worship God and live in total commitment to his laws."[2] Furthermore, the Christian foundations of America are seen in the earliest constitutions such as the Orders of Connecticut written in 1639 and in that of the New England Confederation of May 19, 1643. This latter document begins with these words: "Whereas we all come into these parts of America with one and the same end and aim, namely to advance the Kingdom of our Lord Jesus Christ and to enjoy the liberties of the Gospel in purity with peace . . ."[3]

Second, the American Revolution took place in a Christian context. For example, the journals of the Continental Congress, July 6, 1775 contain these words which give evidence of the religious origins of America's break from Great Britain:

We most solemnly, before God and the world, declare, that, exerting the utmost energy of those powers, which our beneficent Creator hath graciously bestowed upon us, the arms we have been compelled by our enemies to assume, we will, in defiance of every hazard, with unabating firmness and perseverance, employ for the preservation of our liberties; being with one mind resolved to die freemen rather than to live slaves.[4]

Furthermore, before the Revolution the Continental Congress attended services of prayer on July 20, 1775 in Christ Church, Philadelphia. Leaders like Samuel Adams, John Hancock, John Adams, and Patrick Henry all saw the hand of God in the Revolution. Although Falwell recognizes that not all of the fifty-six signers of the Declaration of Independence were Christians, he insists that they were at least strongly influenced by Christian principle. These ideals made them men of "integrity" characterized by "high principles," and "deep moral values." These founders of our country "willingly endured tremendous personal sacrifice to create a nation with the highest ideals of freedom, justice, and morality in the world."[5]

Falwell's third argument for the Christian heritage of America is found in the prayers that attended the formulation and writing of the Constitution of the United States. The representatives of the new nation had struggled for several weeks making little progress. Amid discouragement and confusion Benjamin Franklin rose and called the representatives to prayer. He reminded them of their daily prayers during the contest with Britain and assured them that their prayers had been heard and answered. Franklin challenged the representation to remember the role God had played in the founding of the nation. He asked, "Have we now forgotten this powerful Friend? Or do we imagine we no longer need his assistance?" He then said, "If a sparrow cannot fall to the ground without His notice, is it probable that an empire can rise without His aid?" After admonishing them further that "except the Lord build the house, they labor in vain that build it," he moved that daily prayers precede the business of Congress and adjourned the Congress for two days to seek divine guidance.[6] This stirring speech, remarks Falwell, "marked a turning point in the writing of the Constitution." Consequently, the religious element in the formation of this nation was so strong that George Washington is reported to have said, "It is impossible to rightly govern the world without God and the Bible."[7]

Fourth, the Christian origins of the nation are evident in the First Amendment to the Constitution which states, "Congress shall make no law respecting an establishment of religion, or forbidding the free exercise thereof. . . ." The purpose of this amendment was to prevent the establishment of a state church controlled by the government and supported by taxation. It did not mean, insists Falwell, that "they intended a government devoid of God or of the guidance found in Scripture."[8] Falwell finds support for this view of the First Amendment in the significance the founding fathers gave to God, the scriptures, prayer, and the Ten Commandments.

America Today
The Moral Majority's deep concern about America arises out of their conviction that our country has recently turned away from its spiritual heritage and mission. Consequent-

ly, America desperately needs a revival of religious values.

According to Falwell, evidence abounds that America has turned away from the original vision of the founding fathers. First, the move of our country toward a democracy, especially a socialist democracy where the state ceases to be the servant of man and becomes his master, contradicts the original intent of our founding fathers. They established a republic to prevent the consolidation of power in a centralized government and thus sought to protect the right of every citizen. For example, Falwell asks us to consider the following statement of James Madison:

We have staked the whole future of American civilization not upon the power of government, far from it. We have staked the future of all our political institutions upon the capacity of mankind for self-government; upon the capacity of each and all of us to govern ourselves, to sustain ourselves according to the Ten Commandments of God.[9]

Unfortunately (for Falwell) America has moved toward a centralized and all-encompassing government. Examples of this shift are found in America's faith in a superstate rather than God; in the replacement of Divine Providence by an all-powerful state; and in the abandonment of the Ten Commandments for a state which assumes the prerogative of acting as an ultimate authority in matters of morality. Consequently this country is suffering from an unprecedented moral decline.

Second, because of the faith which many Americans have in government and because of the personal and corporate moral decline of the American people, America is in danger of collapse and takeover by the communist power. Falwell reminds Americans that "the Soviets have always had only one goal, and that is to destroy capitalist society."[10] Consequently, the approach of *detente* represents a dangerous play into the hands of the communists who still intend to bury the free world. American indifference toward Alexander

Solzhenitsyn's passionate plea is a barometer of this country's apathy. This indicates America's willingness to exchange freedom for security—even if that security comes from a communist government. For this reason the Moral Majority is against the Salt II Treaty, the "giving away" of the Panama Canal, and the relationship of America with Taiwan and Mainland China.

Falwell's remedy for this desperate situation is a profound spiritual renewal consisting of a personal conversion by the people of America to Jesus Christ as Lord. Those who are converted need to pray for national repentance, a turning away from sin and moral decay followed by an active involvement in society to return it to its original foundation and calling.[11]

Furthermore, the Moral Majority believes the future of this nation depends on the restoration of American military strength as a deterrent to the spread of communism. Falwell says, "We need leaders of moral courage today who know that there is safety only in strength, not in weakness."[12] Military buildup is the most strategic means to avoid war and the destruction of our world.

In addition to this, Falwell calls for a recovery of purpose in society. In the article "A Cry For Leadership" which appeared in *Time,* August 6, 1979, Falwell approves of the analysis that "our society has become largely purposeless" and that "the task of the nation's leaders in the eighties will be to rediscover new themes of purpose in American life." These new themes are to be found in the Christian faith and in the application of Christian values to the American society. If Americans will return to the founding principles of this country and to the moral convictions which have been recently repudiated, this country has a chance for greatness once again.

Criticism
Much of what the Moral Majority says about the Christian foundations of America is correct, but it does not penetrate

to the heart of the American religious experience. It is certainly true that this nation was founded in the context of religious values, an appeal to God, and a common appeal to the Ten Commandments. It is equally true that the American government has become significantly more pluralistic in the twentieth century, and that in its attempt to represent "all the people" has made decisions which favor a secular rather than theistic view of life. The fears of the Moral Majority are not without a basis in fact.

The difficulty with the Moral Majority view of America is that it is rooted in an American civil religion rather than a true Christian understanding of the place of America in history.

The relationship between religion and the American government from the very beginning has been one of civil religion, not biblical Christianity. The major feature of biblical religion is the centrality of Jesus Christ—his death and resurrection and the presence of his church in the world as the unique presence of the future Kingdom. Civil religion, on the other hand, seldom speaks of Christ and his church. It uses "God-words," referring to dependence on the Almighty, Divine Providence, and the Ten Commandments, but does not contain specific Christian content. It mouths God-words without reference to Jesus Christ.

Robert Linder and Richard Pierard, in their important bicentennial work, *Twilight of the Saints: Biblical Christianity and Civil Religion in America,* define civil religion as "the use of consensus religious sentiments, concepts and symbols by the state—either directly or indirectly, consciously or unconsciously—for its own political purpose."[13]

They point out that although civil religion has been part of the warp and woof of American society from the beginning, it is *not* true Christianity. It is a blending of the Christian faith with national goals and destiny which blurs the distinction between the church and the nation and shifts faith toward a religion of nationalism. In the end this makes the church apostate and creates a counterfeit religion which is a poor substitute for the Christian faith.

What has happened in America in the twentieth century, and especially in the last several decades, is the breakdown of civil religion as the glue which held this nation together under a quasi-Christian morality and external form of religiosity.

What the Moral Majority is calling for, perhaps unknowingly, is a restoration of civil religion. This is more evident in Falwell's admission that "we count among us Fundamentalists, Protestants, Roman Catholics, Jews, Mormons, and *persons of no particular religious convictions at all who believe in the moral principles we espouse*"[14] (emphasis added). In this same article there is no mention of Jesus Christ and the uniqueness of the church as the true source of values in society. Thus, what the Moral Majority espouses is a morality based on civil religion, not on the unique revelation of God in the person and work of Jesus Christ.

Chapter Four

Moralism

The media attention given to the Moral Majority leaves the impression that theirs is a one-issue campaign. Nothing could be further from the truth. The word "morality" embraces a complex web of issues which affect almost every aspect of American society. These issues may be arranged under three general headings: *underlying issues; means of deterioration; effects on society.*

Underlying Issues
Falwell and other Moral Majority leaders have identified four basic problems which permeate our entire culture. These problems lie beneath the surface of our declining society. They are *secular humanism, centralized government, moral decadence,* and the *crisis of leadership.*

First, it is generally recognized that *secular humanism* has become the dominant world view. Secular humanism is a philosophy of life which seeks to understand and interpret all of life without reference to God. This view of life results from the breakdown of the Christian or God-centered world view held in the ancient church and by the Reformers. The slide toward secularism began with the radical humanists of the Renaissance and gradually, through the last four centuries, infiltrated every area of human thought and action.

The philosophy of secular humanism has been articulated in two documents known as *Humanist Manifesto I* written in 1933 and *Humanist Manifesto II* which was published in 1973. Many of America's public leaders, philosophers, writers, educators, and others in areas of influence subscribe to the tenets of secular humanism articulated in these documents.

Secular humanism denies the existence of the supernatural and subscribes to naturalism and materialism (as a philosophical concept). This viewpoint tends to absolutize human beings and rules out the possibility of any ultimate point of reference outside the material world. This is what Francis Schaeffer calls a "closed world view system." In this system revelation is rejected and the human mind raised to a position of ultimacy. The consequence is that humans must become the arbiter of moral law. Humans must determine through consensus or the rule of the elite what is morally right or wrong.

Furthermore, the denial of persons as image-bearers of God makes humans a "kind of animal." Although most humanists insist on the intrinsic value of persons, the failure to recognize the transcendent quality of human life leaves the door open to the devaluation of persons as in abortion, euthanasia, and genetic manipulation. Humanism also fails to provide an object system of ethics leaving the door open to the sexual revolution where "anything goes."

In short, secular humanism has no means of providing a universal authoritative interpretation of life. Thus, the adherence to humanism whether directly and consciously or indirectly and unconsciously by the American public has undermined the meaning, significance, and purpose of life. Contemporary Americans are thus left in a world void of meaning and vulnerable to a totalitarian takeover by the elite who will assign their own meaning to morality.

The second underlying issue is the problem of a *centralized government*. It is a major concern to the Moral Majority that America has "embraced the very centralized government the Founding Fathers urged them to fear and hold in check."[1] Falwell laments the growth of thousands of bureaucracies which destroy the productivity of the institutions they supervise and the increasing antibusiness attitude of Congress.

For Falwell, freedom is directly related to the free enterprise system. Because America has progressively abandoned the principles of the free enterprise system for an all-embracing government, Americans have "exchanged freedom for security and welfarism has become an increasing burden to the state."[2]

The third underlying concern which Falwell and the Moral Majority articulate is the permeating presence of *moral decadence*. Morality, which is rooted in the Ten Commandments and the Bible, is in a state of erosion because the leaders of this country have replaced moral absolutes with permissiveness. Falwell says:

We are very quickly moving toward an amoral society where nothing is either absolutely right or absolutely wrong. Our absolutes are disappearing, and with this disappearance we must face the sad fact that our society is crumbling.[3]

Falwell feels so strongly about the loss of moral nerve in our culture that he can call it the "root of America's problems today."[4] The all-pervasive permissiveness spawned by secular humanism lurks beneath the major moral issues of our time. We can trace all our problems back to the loss of morality: the breakdown of the family; abortion; juvenile delinquency; promiscuity; drug addiction; economic and political chaos; and a weak defense posture. For this reason Falwell finds himself in agreement with the words of General Douglas MacArthur:

History fails to record a single precedent in which nations subject to moral decay have not passed into political and economic decline. There has been either a spiritual awakening to overcome the moral lapse or a progressive deterioration leading to ultimate national disaster.[5]

Consequently, Falwell believes the 1980s is the time to turn America around. He believes that these next ten years will be "the most important decade this nation has ever known."[6]

This brings us to the fourth major problem, namely the *crisis of leadership*. The drift into the purposelessness of secular humanism, the apathy created by a centralized government, and the loss of a positive moral direction in our society has led to a sense of national "lostness." Tragically, there is a lack of leaders to grasp the situation and lead us out of this morass of uncertainty.

The kind of leadership needed today is Christian leadership—a leadership which will bring this country "back to basics, back to values, back to biblical morality, back to sensibility, and back to patriotism." This leadership has to come from "the highest places in every level of government," but this alone will not be sufficient to turn America around. Leadership must also come from the people who "have been lax in voting in and out of office the right and the wrong people." The hope of turning this country around lies with the Christian public—a public which is informed of our current crisis, convinced of the critical moment of our time, and prepared to give and demand moral leadership.[7]

Means of Deterioration
According to the Moral Majority, these forces of debilitation are being spread primarily through the following means: *public education, television,* and the *popular arts*.

First, *public education* is committed to secular humanism.

According to Falwell, humanistic public education has replaced a commitment to factual knowledge with a stress on students' "social and psychological growth." Consequently, "socialization" has become the major purpose of public education. Since secular humanism proclaims no moral absolutes students are left to develop their own value systems. The result is that most American young people develop a creed of life which affirms that "moral values are relative" and that "ethics are situational."[8]

Furthermore, these secular humanists find a ready avenue of infiltration through the educational textbooks. Falwell comments:

From kindergarten right through the total school system, it almost seems as if classroom textbooks are designed to negate what philosophies previously had been taught. Under the guise of sex education or value clarification many textbooks are actually perverting the minds of literally millions of students.[9]

One such textbook is *Human Sexuality: A Course For Young Adults*. This book was approved by the California State Board of Education and is used in some school systems in the seventh and eighth grade. Sex is explicitly presented in both words and pictures. More than that, the book pokes fun at traditional views of sex and informs the student that "disapproval of pre-marital sexual activity is not shared by the majority of the world's cultures." According to Falwell the book condones infidelity and takes up subjects such as "homosexuality, incest, masochism, masturbation, sadism, and nymphomania."[10]

Another textbook titled *Man: A Course of Study* (MACOS) was produced by the National Science Foundation under the leadership of Jerome Bruner, Harvard psychologist in experimental behavior. This book contains a programmed humanism not only in the text, but also in questions and answers from which the teacher and student

may not deviate. These books and others like them which
have become standardized textbooks in public schools lead
Falwell to conclude "that public education has become
materialistic, humanistic, atheistic, and socialistic." This
situation is a "far cry from what our Founding Fathers
intended education to be."[11]

Second, Falwell sees *television* as one of the major instruments through which the breakdown of society is mirrored
and aided. Like education, television has been captured by
secular humanism. It operates without absolutes and standards. "Television," writes Falwell, "is brainwashing children, young people, and adults to accept an amoral life
style."[12] The alarming feature of television is that it is "the
most powerful medium in the world today. It is a molder
of attitudes, of behavior, and of taste." Because it "can
capture the mind, the attention and the imagination of people" it can be used for good or evil. Therefore, the question
of television is an "ethical issue."[13]

One of the major problems Americans concerned about
public morality must face is the amoral impact which television is making on society. Falwell—and here he is joined
by many others—sees a network commitment to programs
which titillate the baser instincts of immorality and violence
because this is what attracts the largest following and draws
the highest ratings. Furthermore, because television has become the "largest baby-sitting agency in the world," our
children are learning their moral values through this
medium. Even the advertising to which we are constantly
subjected is "replete with sexual images."[14]

Much television programming suffers from insipidity.
Worse, it often portrays an idealized lifestyle—one that is
materialistic, sensual, exotic, and jet-set oriented. Consequently, we are incessantly bombarded with negative images and values which hasten our society's slide toward
decadence.

The third force which is contributing to the breakdown

of American culture is the *popular arts*. Although some movies and contemporary art could be cited as examples, Falwell chooses contemporary rock music as his prime example in this area.

He sees rock music as the servant of secular humanism, but even more as a medium for satanic influence. Although this charge could be made of many rock groups, it is particularly true of the Rolling Stones. Their record *Goats Head Soup* was reputedly recorded at a live voodoo ritual. The screams heard on the record are of those who are "allegedly being possessed by demon spirits." In addition, the Rolling Stones have a number of other albums dedicated to Satanism such as *Their Satanic Majesty's Request* in which they appear on the cover dressed as witches. Of this group David Dalton in his book *Rock One Hundred* says they "actually seem" to be "the ringleaders of an international conspiracy of rock 'n' roll punks to undermine Western civilization with drugs, music, polymorphous sexuality, and violence."[15]

Falwell objects not only to the lyrics but to the sound of rock music. He quotes Bob Larson, a converted rock musician, who claims:

By its very beat and sound, rock has always implicitly rejected restraints and celebrated moral anarchy. Its repetitious and pulsating rhythms mesmerize the listener and induce a state of moral oblivion. The beat of rock, with amplified intensity, encourages a feeling of complete abandonment of accepted social behavior. The electronic insistence of guitars, accompanied by the neurotic throbbing of drums, compels the shedding of inhibitions.[16]

For this reason rock music feeds into and promotes sexual promiscuity, drugs, and the occult. Tragically, these rock stars are the heroes of American young people. Thus the examples they provide and the positions they promote become vehicles for the landslide of moral decadence that threatens to engulf this country.

Effects on Society

Jerry Falwell and the Moral Majority point to at least four effects which result from the concerns outlined above. They include the *breakdown of the family;* the *homosexual revolution; pornography;* and the *spread and pervasiveness of drugs.*

First, the *breakdown of the family* is directly related to the larger environmental situation in America. According to Falwell, secular humanism has clearly played a significant role in the disruption of the family. He sees a "vicious assault upon the American family" coming largely from television. Increased programming depicting homes of divorced and single family parents as normal indirectly attacks the traditional family structure. Many of these TV programs openly justify "divorce, homosexuality, and adultery."[17] Consequently, the commitment among the young to life-long marriages, to fidelity, and the nuclear family is on the decline. If this condition continues to worsen the nuclear family as the norm may soon disappear.

Two additional factors contributing to the breakdown of the family are the playboy philosophy and feminism. *Playboy* is more than a dirty magazine—it is a philosophy of life which "represents a life style that ultimately corrupts the family. Men are satisfying their lustful desires at the expense of the family." Feminists also promote an unmoral lifestyle. Their commitment is to "get out and do my own thing," to "have my own dirty magazines," to "self-satisfaction" which they regard as "more important than the family."[18]

The government also threatens the family. Its recent attempt to redefine the family is a major concern of the Moral Majority. The establishment of the White House Conference on Families (1980), while ostensibly a move in a positive direction, has produced negative results because of the persons assigned to the commission and the results to which they came. For example, "it was decided that any persons living together constituted a family."[19] While this definition could include two homosexual men or two lesbians living together, it was justified on the assumption that it more perfectly reflects current "differences in structure and life style." (Against such antifamily forces a profamily movement has emerged.) In this instance Falwell sees the forces of humanism, government, and moral decadence working together to destroy the God-ordained family as the basic social unit of society. He approvingly quotes Senator Helms: "we must restore and preserve the family as the focus of our personal and social well-being and the strongest defense we have against the totalitarian state."[20]

The next result of America's spiritual decadence is the rise and spread of the *homosexual revolution*. Falwell regards the biblical teaching against homosexuality to be unequivocal. It is rejected not only in the Old Testament (Lev. 18:22; 20:13) but also in the New Testament (Rom. 1:26-28; I Cor. 6:9, 10; I Tim. 1:9). He believes that "a person is not born with preference to the same sex, but he is introduced to the homosexual experience and cultivates a homosexual urge. It is innocent children and young people who are victimized and who become addicts to sexual perversion."[21]

Secular humanism cannot help homosexuals and, as a matter of fact, ends up giving support to their lifestyle since it has no absolute and transcendent value by which to evaluate the homosexual urge.

Consequently, the government, because it has been influenced by an amoral secularism, is at a loss to know how to deal with the issue. There is a current bill in Congress (H.R. 2074) which, if passed, "would establish homosexuals in America as a bona fide minority like women, blacks, Hispanics, etc." The consequence of this bill would be to force employers to "employ a minority of homosexuals commensurate with the population in their area." Falwell fears the "flaunting of homosexual life style" which would be "detrimental to the basic tenet of Christian society, the home."[22]

A third pervasive problem is the rise of *pornography*. The freedom which has been given to the pornographers is a result of secular humanism and its failure to have an absolute standard. Consequently, the sexual revolution and permissiveness runs rampant throughout our society.

Even the government is incapable of handling the problem because it has no standard by which to judge pornography. Thus, Falwell comments:

Our judicial system judges human sexuality by a man-determined code of sexual conduct, not by the Word of God. In 1973 it was decided, by a divided U.S. Supreme Court in the case Miller vs. California, that communities must decide what constitutes obscenity.[23]

Pornography debilitates. First, it is a "form of enslavement" because it locks a person into lust and evil. Second, it "displays a distorted view of women." It degrades women by turning them into mere sex objects to be used and abused by the perverse sexual desires of depraved men. Third, it "destroys the privacy of sex." Pornography goes beyond the mere sex act to display acts of violence where women are "tortured, devoured, and mutilated." Furthermore, pornography which involves children is a form of "child abuse" which cannot be tolerated. Consequently, Christians must see that pornography "is more than a nudie magazine, it is a prevailing atmosphere of sexual license."[24]

Finally, the *spread and pervasiveness of drugs* presents a frightening spectacle of where this country is going. Francis Schaeffer in *How Should We Then Live?* points out that many young people have turned to drugs as a symptom of the meaninglessness of our time and an expression of their desire to escape the reality of a world in chaos.

The spread of drugs in America is considerably more

extensive and frightening than most people imagine. Congressman Lester Wolff, Chairman of the House of Representatives Select Committee on Narcotics Abuse and Control has pointed out the following:

Not only is the United States the most pervasive drug abusing nation in history, but drug abuse among our children has risen, in the past two years, from epidemic to pandemic proportions. It has grown so large that neither this nation—nor any nation in history—has ever before faced a problem that is so insidious and so dangerous. And if we don't recognize the importance of this problem, it will have disastrous effects upon our society.[25]

Criticism

Most centrists would not find much fault with Falwell's analysis of the moral ills of society. He has touched on a number of issues which have surfaced in this country recently—issues which concern most religious people, and especially those who are concerned about the erosion of morals and values.

However, there are two issues which the Moral Majority must face in the near future. One is the need to have a more inclusive ethic, the other is the question of whether the Moral Majority will represent a mere return to civil religion or a call to a radical commitment to Jesus Christ and his church.

First, Falwell scarcely mentions the problems of the poor people and minorities, the problem of discrimination, the establishment of justice, concern for the hungry, and issues of energy and environment. Nor does he talk of crisis pregnancy centers, rehabilitation centers for alcoholics and drug abusers, medical and legal clinics for the poor, and food and clothing outlets for the needy. Nevertheless, much of this kind of work already exists at Thomas Road Baptist Church in Lynchburg. Furthermore, his most recent public speeches indicate that he is going to turn his attention and that of the Moral Majority to these issues. He is prompted to move in this direction both by Christian compassion and by the desire to take welfare away from the government and give it back to the church. This vision is commendable, and centrists are in wholehearted support of these new efforts.

However, an issue still remains. Will this work be done in the name of Christ and his church? Or will it compromise the far-reaching demands of Christ by failing to see the antithesis between the church as the redeemed society and government as part of the fallen order? Failure to make that distinction could very well lead to the restoration of civil religion.

The Moral Majority will have to face this temptation because there are many fundamentalists and evangelicals who have so thoroughly confused civil religion with true Christianity that it is hard to tell the difference.

America has become increasingly pagan and materialistic. A Christianity that continues to regard this country a "chosen nation" has two choices: accommodation to national goals, or change through force. The former is apostasy, the latter is fascism.

Robert Linder and Richard Pierard in their book *Twilight of the Saints* set forth five arguments against civil religion. These need to be heard by the Moral Majority. They are: (1) cohabitation with civil religion leaves the false impression that the nation, not Christ, saves; (2) civil religion can be used as a tool by national leaders to drum up support for questionable policies; (3) the church which accommodates itself to civil religion makes it nearly impossible to challenge the values of American culture; (4) civil religion reduces the God of the universe to the status of a tribal God; (5) civil religion may become a vehicle of national self-righteousness and idolatry.[26]

There is a better way—to develop a proper understanding of the church and to effect change by means of its proclamation of the gospel; its witness as a true Christian community—a "society within the society"; its personal and corporate radical obedience to the values, norms, and morals given to it by Jesus Christ; and its witness to the state and other aspects of the social order through mediating institutions. In this way, the church, which is God's chosen people throughout the world will transcend national programs and boundaries and witness to Christ as Lord in meaningful and concrete ways.

This does not mean that Christians cannot be good citizens. As Linder and Pierard point out genuine patriots love their native soil, affirm the future, ascribe to diversity, are willing to serve, and affirm the primacy of God over all things. The ultimate loyalty of the Christian lies with Jesus Christ. Nevertheless, the Christian is called to be a good citizen (Rom. 13), to give the government its due place in his or her life, and to support the government except in those areas where it requires Christians to compromise their ethic and ultimate allegiance to Christ as Lord.

Part II

Turn to the Left:
The World Council of Churches

Chapter Five

Socialism

This section, is intended to show that the approach of the World Council of Churches has many similarities to that of the Moral Majority. Like the Moral Majority the WCC is attached to a particular economic system, views America with a specific bias, and delineates its social agenda in keeping with its economic predisposition. Its major difference with the Moral Majority is that it affirms the flip side of the coin, emphasizing economic socialism, American oppression, and liberation theology as opposed to capitalism, America as a chosen nation, and moralism.

Background
When liberal Protestants began to preach their social gospel in earnest during the early decades of the twentieth century, fundamentalists backed away from social issues leaving that area entirely to the liberals. Thus a split developed in American Protestantism between fundamentalists who believed in personal faith and individual piety and liberals who believed in the corporate church as the instrument of social justice. The rift between the two camps became so wide that many denominations split over the issue.

In the meantime this country turned to the left in the New Deal introduced by President Franklin Delano

Roosevelt. This was a conscious move away from the free enterprise system toward a more socialistic form of government.

It was the mainline liberal church which jumped on the bandwagon and quickly approved of these policies, seeing within them an ally for Christian social action. For this reason the liberal church embraced socialistic economics. The ideology of liberal social ethics is therefore drawn from a combination of biblical passages with a socialist or (more recently for some extremists) Marxist agenda. The prophetic center is as opposed to this ideology as it is to that of the civil religion agenda of the Moral Majority.

A Straightforward Biblical Base

The left, like the right, is built on select passages of scripture. These scriptures have to do with the biblical concern for justice and righteousness—the concern of Jesus—for the poor. The major theme is that of liberation from the oppressor—a theme which uses the Exodus as its prime example. Here are a few examples:

1. concern for justice

> For I know how many are your transgressions,
> and how great are your sins–
> you who afflict the righteous, who take a bribe,
> and turn aside the needy in the gate.
> Therefore he who is prudent will keep silent in such a time;
> for it is an evil time.
>
> Seek good, and not evil
> that you may live;
> and so the Lord, the God of hosts, will be with you,
> as you have said.
> Hate evil, and love good,
> and establish justice in the gate;
> it may be that the Lord, the God of hosts
> will be gracious to the remnant of Joseph.
>
> –Amos 5:12-15

2. *the concern of Jesus for the poor*

> The Spirit of the Lord is upon me,
> because he has anointed me to preach good news to the poor.
> He has sent me to proclaim release to the captives
> and recovering of sight to the blind,
> to set at liberty those who are oppressed,
> to proclaim the acceptable year of the Lord.
>
> –Luke 4:18-19

3. *the Exodus theme of liberation*

> Say therefore to the people of Israel,
> 'I am the Lord, and I will bring you out from
> under the burdens of the Egyptians, and I will
> deliver you from their bondage, and I will
> redeem you with an outstretched arm and
> with great acts of judgment, and I will
> take you for my people, and I will be
> your God; and you shall know that I
> am the Lord, your God, who has brought
> you out from the burdens of the Egyptians.'
>
> —Exodus 6:6-7

Scripture Interpreted Through the Ideals of Socialism

It has already been mentioned that liberal Christianity took over the social programs of the American church, and found a bedfellow in the growing interest in socialism.[1]

Socialism seeks to put the benefits of industrial wealth into the hands of the worker, either through governmental legislation or by cooperative ownership of industry. It does not necessarily advocate equal income, nor does it mean political dictatorship. It is an economic system that looks at wealth from the side of the poor.

The relationship between socialism and communism is often misunderstood. They are not the same. It is true that Karl Marx saw socialism as a step toward communism. But communism promotes dictatorship and the denial of civil liberties—a viewpoint which socialists vigorously reject. Therefore, democratic socialists regard communism as a state capitalism and reject it as a goal.

In this country socialism was strongest after World War I. In 1904 its membership was 400,000; in 1921, 900,000; and by 1924 the socialist vote was about a million in strength. It was in this context that the nineteenth-century Ritschlian school of theology became prominent. Ritschl's main point was that the ethical teachings of Christianity were meant for society as a whole. This value-oriented Christianity found its most significant prophetic voice in the social writings of Walter Rauschenbusch, especially his work *A Theology for the Social Gospel*. Rauschenbusch took the ideas of Ritschl and popularized them for a Christian church which was becoming increasingly attuned to the growing plight of the cities and the spread of sin through the institutions of man. Here, for example, is a classic statement of his thesis.

Sin is essentially selfishness. That definition is more in harmony with the social gospel than with any individualistic type of religion. The sinful mind, then, is the unsocial and anti-social mind. To find the climax of sin we must not linger over a man who swears, or sneers at religion, or denies the mystery of the trinity, but put our hands on social groups who have turned the patrimony of a nation into the private property of a small class, or have left the peasant labourers cowed, degraded, demoralized, and without rights in the land. When we find such in history, or in present-day life, we shall know we have struck real rebellion against God on the higher levels of sin.[2]

This point of view grew rapidly among other theologians and church leaders as the mainline church rapidly oriented itself toward societal change as the means of witnessing to the progressive presence of the Kingdom of God.

Marxist Interpretation of the Church's Social Mission
Reinhold Niebuhr was one of the outstanding theologians

of our century and a strong supporter of the socialist agenda. Although he was no friend of communism, he was one of the first theologians to recognize the significance of the Marxist critique of society for the social program of the church. In his most significant political work, *Moral Man and Immoral Society,* he wrote that Marxism "made no mistake in stating the rational goal toward which society must move, the goal of equal justice, or in understanding the economic foundations of justice."[3]

Consequently, Niebuhr and others following him increasingly endorsed the Marxist critique. They believed capitalism should be replaced by social ownership of the means of production, the sole hope for a just society in a technical age.[4] These ideas became ascendant in liberal Christianity and increasingly informed the social agenda of the National Council of Churches and the World Council of Churches.

Many Christian leaders saw an affinity between Christianity and Marxism and sought to forge an unusual alliance between the two, particularly in Latin America. This alliance is testified to by Jose Miguez Bonino, of the World Council of Churches, in his book *Christians and Marxists* in the following words:

Perhaps it is just as well that I state explicitly from the very beginning the presuppositions from which this book is written. Some readers may thus be spared the effort of reading further. Others may be helped to put what they read in perspective.

This book is written from the point of view of a person who confesses Jesus Christ as his Lord and Saviour. This is his centre of gravity and everything else is seen (in intention, at least) in relation to it. The reality and power of the Triune God, the witness of Holy Scriptures, the story of God's salvation are not seen as hypotheses to be proved, but as the foundation of life, action, understanding and hope. This presupposition belongs, to be sure, to the realm of faith and therefore can only be justified eschatologically, when faith becomes sight, 'and all men shall see him.'

A second presupposition belongs to the level of history; as a Latin American Christian I am convinced—with many other Latin Americans who have tried to understand the situation of our people and to place it in world perspective—that revolutionary action aimed at changing the basic economic, political, social, and cultural structures and conditions of life is imperative today in the world. Ours is not a time for mere development, rearranging or correction, but for basic and revolutionary change (which ought not to be equated necessarily with violence). The possibility for human life to remain human on our planet hangs on our ability to effect this change. Such a conviction can only partially be justified in discussion: convictions in the area of history can be theoretically explained but they can only be proved practically—by turning them into history.

Still in another level lies the presupposition—which I shall try to argue throughout the book—that the socioanalytical tools, the historical horizon of interpretation, the insight into the dynamics of the social process and the revolutionary ethos and programme which Marxism has either received and appropriated or itself created are, however corrected or reinterpreted, indispensable for revolutionary change.

To bring together these vastly different presuppositions is the task to which I shall try to make a very small contribution.[5]

Liberal Christian Social Action Dominated by Liberation Themes

Since 1970 the word liberation has been attached to a new "theology of liberation." In that year the publication of Peruvian Gustavo Gutierrez's work *The Theology of Liberation* caught the attention of theologians around the world. The main burden of his theology is one which goes beyond mere reflection, one which

. . . tries to be part of the process through which the world is transformed. It is theology which is open—in the protest against trampled human dignity, in the struggle against the plunder of the vast majority of people, in liberating love, and in the building of a new, just and fraternal society—to the gift of the Kingdom of God.[6]

At the fifth assembly of the World Council of Churches held in Nairobi (November 23-December 10, 1975), liberation was a major theme. An example may be taken from the major address given by Michael Manley, former Prime Minister of Jamaica. Part of his speech included a strong denunciation of capitalism. He said, "At no point in history has an economic system reflected the process of domination in political, social, psychological, and ultimately even in philosophical terms more completely than under capitalism."[7] David Patton's report goes on to say, "Mr. Manley ended his address with an eloquent appeal for action to liberate the victims of oppression now; and was greeted with a prolonged standing ovation."[8]

In 1978 the noted American theologian Robert McAfee Brown published his work, *Theology in a New Key: Responding to Liberation Themes*. In this well-received work, he calls on American Christians to recognize the importance of the liberation theme and to join in political action which will affirm and establish human rights.

This theme of liberation which can be traced through the Marxist critique and the interest in socialism is finally rooted in the biblical concern for the poor, the oppressed, and the weak. It forms the underlying ideological basis of the leaders of the more liberal mainline Protestant and Catholic churches.

Criticism
The problem with the social ethics of the World Council of Churches is similar to that of the Moral Majority. It supports socialism and Marxism as though they alone are the economic and political systems through which God is doing his work in the world. Like the Moral Majority the WCC fails to have a Christocentric understanding of the

church and ends up accommodating the vision of the Kingdom to the goals of an earthly power.

For this reason the first criticism against the WCC is that it has prepared the way for the goals of the church to be united with a "Christianized" version of Marxism. It justifies this approach because of the failure of previous strategies. Specifically, liberal Christianity identifies five areas of breakdown which have prepared the way for a Marxist-Christian convergence.

First, some in the church have been guilty of privatizing the faith, making it a matter of personal intellectual theory or private personal ethics which have no relation to the social issues of life. Second, others have been guilty of spiritualizing the faith, making it a religion only of the "other world," lifting it out of the plane of historical realism. Third, the liberals of the church have been guilty of relativizing faith and morals so greatly that the church appears to have lost all doctrinal, moral, or social definiteness. Fourth, these conditions have resulted in "a church without purpose." The church appears to be weak, bland, and irresolute. Fifth, the American church is essentially more theoretical than practical. For this reason it has been characterized by unreality in the face of modern world problems and needs. It is interesting that these criticisms can be directed especially against a naturalistic liberalism which has reduced the church to little more than another human institution. No wonder the leadership has turned to Marxism, one of the most driving forces for change in the world today.

A second criticism against the WCC is that Christianity and Marxism represent two entirely different world views which cannot be synthesized. "Marxist Christianity" is neither Christian nor Marxist; it is merely an amalgam that destroys what is distinctive about each.

Marxism is an all-embracing ideology. It has its own comprehensive world view, interpretation of human history, and agenda for every sphere of life. In this sense it is a "kind of religion." It is grounded in a materialistic view of the origin of the world; it contains a doctrine of sin (the class struggle); it offers a view of salvation (redemption by the proletariat from oppression); it has a goal for humanity (the gradual creation of a classless society and the emergence of the golden era of communism).[7]

Marxism hopes to win the future by putting its theories into practice, thus transforming people, nations, and cultures to achieve a new society. On the individual level this can be accomplished by putting away personal commitments to "selfishness" and becoming a new person through the transformation of character. This same process occurs within nations—sometimes by revolution.

The sharp distinction between Marxism and Christianity is apparent in the Marxist agenda for humanity. Marxists place their hope in the ability of human persons to bring about the revolution toward human maturity and to maintain it once achieved.

True Christianity believes that God alone is the Savior of humankind and that salvation has already occurred in Jesus Christ, is now extended in the universal society of the church, and will be consummated in the second coming of Christ. The unique feature of Christian hope is that it comes from the divine side and will be accomplished only by Jesus Christ at the consummation of history.

Consequently, the confluence between Christianity and Marxism is an ideological impossibility. At best it will make the church apostate and at worst, should Marxism succeed, it will turn against the church and seek to destroy it. The church cannot make a holy alliance with an unholy power without compromising its true character as the radical and unique universal society of people called to be the presence of the future in the world now. The WCC has compromised the true character of the church as a divine institution by aligning it with the agenda of socialist and communist revolutions. The answer to poverty and discrimination does not lie in a particular economic or political position, but in the church as the new community of people who speak in the name of Jesus and live out his life in the world. The universal church must find new and creative ways to make Christ present in the community of the faithful and to mediate this presence to oppressive structures without becoming corrupted by them.

Chapter Six

Minority Groups

The predisposition of the World Council of Churches toward the Marxist critique and a liberation theology naturally leads the left to view America from the viewpoint of the underdog.

It is a fact that to certain people the American nation looks more like the devil than the savior. There are the minorities who feel oppressed by the American system. For them the flag does not emote the positive sentiments it does for the white person. What they want is to be freed from the economic and political shackles of their imprisonment in a society that has acted without liberty and justice to them.

Martin E. Marty, in his work, *The Pro and Con Book of Religious America* (a bicentennial special), clearly demonstrated to his readers that there is more than one way to look at America. In the *pro* side Marty emphasizes all the aspects of American history that the right would have us remember. In the *con* side Marty shows the other side of the coin—the dark side of American history that the left wants to emphasize.

The dark side is characterized by many unpleasant themes such as materialism, an anti-historical spirit, lonely individualism, provincialism, prejudice, racism, and male domination.

There is an increasing interest among many religious leaders to be honest about this side of America. This is, partly if not largely, the result of the minority voices which have surfaced in recent years. Historians, theologians, and civic leaders from the minority communities want to know more about the history of their group and how it fits into the overall pattern of American history. What the minority groups have discovered is not altogether pleasant, and the presentation of their findings to the American public shows the complicity of the American church in some very embarrassing attitudes and actions.

According to the ideology of the World Council of Churches, God is at work in those historically grounded movements which intend either by peaceful or violent means to release the oppressed from the oppressor. A similar approach has been applied to the American Revolution, by the Moral Majority. However, while the Moral Majority stops with a providential view of the American Revolution, the WCC advocates the continuing liberation of all oppressed people with God at the center acting to "save" the oppressed from the oppressor. Three such examples of liberation movements in the United States can be drawn from the Indians, the blacks, and women.

The Indians: God Is Red
Recently, a number of books have been published about American Indians and the subsequent treatment they received in the formation of this nation. The most popular of these is probably Dee Brown's *Bury My Heart at Wounded Knee* and the two anthologies of Indian speeches, *I Have Spoken* and *Touch the Earth*. The most significant indictment of Christian America, however, is *God Is Red* by Vine Deloria, Jr. There are three themes which seem central to his analysis.

First, Deloria points to a significant difference between an Indian and American Christian view of land. The choice is, he suggests, "between conceiving of land as either a subject or an object."[1] The Indian sees land as a subject; nature is not something "wild," but something "mysterious." He quotes chief Luther Standing Bear:

To us it was tame. Earth was bountiful and we were surrounded with the blessings of the Great Mystery. Not until the hairy man from the east came and with brutal frenzy heaped injustices upon us and the families that we loved was it "wild" for us. When the very animals of the forest began fleeing from his approach, then it was that for us the "Wild West" began.[2]

Second, Deloria speaks of the "invasion" of the land by the settlers. He sees the westward movement as an expression of violence in which both the land and the people became the "victims of Christian peoples."[3]

This violence against the people and the land was motivated by "unmitigated greed."[4] Deloria traces the religious sanction of the seizure of land to the *Inter Caetera* bull of Pope Alexander VI, issued in 1493, which set forth the basic Christian attitude toward the new world. Among other things the bull promoted the notion that "barbarous nations be overthrown and brought to the faith itself." What this "pious language meant in practical terms was that if confiscation of lands were couched in quasi-religious sentiments, the nations of Europe could proceed."[5]

Gradually this doctrine of the Pope allowed the natives to be "classified as those who had meant to be subjugated" and was soon "secularized into justification for European nations, definitively Christian, to conquer and subdue the peoples of the lands which they entered."[6]

For this reason, Deloria interprets American history as one of colonization and exploitation, and he sees the church, both Catholic and Protestant, as involved in the process. So far as he is concerned, "it was only when people were able to combine Western greed with religious fanaticism that the type and extent of exploitation that history has recorded was made possible."[7]

Nevertheless, Deloria does recognize that the United States has at least set up a claims commission to "rectify treaty wrongs with the native inhabitants" while Canada and Australia have refused to do so. In reply to those Christians who say, "but the people who did this were not really Christian," he asks, "Why did not the true Christians rise up in defiance of the derogation of their (the Indians') religious heritage and faith?"[8]

Here we have a view of America that is diametrically opposed to that of the Moral Majority. For the Indians America is the perpetuator of evil, not the divine "chosen nation." Consequently, the left looks at America through the eyes of the Indian and sees God at work justifying and liberating an oppressed people. The same principle is true for the blacks.

The Blacks: God Is Black

The plight of blacks in America was greatly dramatized by the civil rights movement of the 1960s. Since that time interest in the origins of slavery and the history of blacks in America has been rekindled. *Roots,* the best-selling book by Alex Haley and the subsequent television series based on the book, has brought the treatment of the black in America to the attention of every American.

It is a sad fact that at the time this nation was being "conceived in liberty and dedicated to the proposition that all men are created equal," twenty percent of its population was being held in slavery. Patriotic Americans had gone to war to protect freedom; yet when the Declaration of Independence was signed twenty million blacks were slaves of "free men." Evangelical Christians were, for the most part, supportive of slavery. The Southern Presbyterian J. H.

Thornwell said, "The Scriptures not only fail to condemn slavery . . . they as distinctly sanction it as any other social condition of man." Even George Whitefield, the great itinerant preacher of America's first Great Awakening in the 1740s, "proposed that slavery be introduced into the new colony of Georgia, where it had been originally forbidden, so that his much-acclaimed orphanage might reap the benefits."[9]

Several black theologians have attempted to come to grips with the history of blacks in America to develop a "black theology." The best known black theologians are James H. Cone, *God of the Oppressed* and Sterling Tucker, *Black Reflections on White Power*. Tucker dwells more on the actual experience of blacks at the hands of whites, so we will draw four points from his work that seem most pertinent to an understanding of blacks in American society.[10]

In the first place, it is evident that blacks were not valued as persons, and for that reason were deprived of their freedom. From the very first, when they were captured and taken from their homeland, little or no thought whatsoever was given to their right to life, and to their pursuit of happiness with family and friends in their own tribal setting. The atrocities against their right to a full human life began immediately after their capture. Gustavas Vasa, an enslaved African, describes in agonizing detail his deprivation from freedom in his trip to America in these words:

I would have jumped over the side, but I could not; and besides, the crew used to watch us very closely who were not chained down to the decks, lest we should leap into the water: and I have seen some of these poor African prisoners most severely cut for attempting to do so, and hourly whipped for not eating. This indeed was often the case with myself.[11]

Second, the denial of freedom expressed itself in the American unwillingness to protect black family rights. It was not uncommon to sell a husband to one master and a wife to another. Children were frequently severed from their parents and sent to other masters where they were deprived knowledge of or contact with their parents. Young people contemplating marriage could not be certain of a life-long marriage with their partner and the benefit of a loving family. Marriages between slaves were not even recognized as law. In 1858 a North Carolina judge wrote:

The relation between slaves is essentially different from that of man and wife joined in lawful wedlock . . . (for) with slaves it may be dissolved at the pleasure of either party, or by the sale of one or both, depending on the caprice or necessity of the owners.[12]

In the third place the culture, customs, and history of the blacks were taken away from them. Tucker claims that "slaves were forced to adopt the white man's religion, the white man's customs, the white man's mode of dress, the white man's value system." Consequently, anything black was "frowned upon." Blacks were encouraged to become "white" in their behavior, "to look with shame on their dark, uncivilized homelands."[13]

Next, the slaveholders, having "Americanized" the blacks, refused them education. In some states slaveholders were instrumental in passing laws which forbade slave education. Alabama, for example, "levied $250 to $500 fines on anyone who taught a slave or even a free black to read or write." In Mississippi anyone who attempted to teach a black "could be fined $30, be put in jail for ten days, or receive 39 lashes." In North Carolina it was deemed a criminal act to distribute "any pamphlet or book, not ex-cluding the Bible" to blacks. Consequently, when slavery was finally abolished, "Blacks were still separated from all that was black and noble in their pasts." Even though attempts are now being made to recognize the place and importance of blacks in American history, black history is still looked upon as something *outside* American history—a separate history not yet understood and interpreted in its interrelationship with all the other facets of American events and historical periods of time.[14]

A case in point is the interpretation of the Civil War and the role of Abraham Lincoln. While Lincoln is celebrated as the one who emancipated the blacks, they themselves see Lincoln differently. According to Tucker he "did not free the slaves because he felt slavery to be a grave moral injustice." Rather he freed the slaves because "he was a pragmatist; his goal was to save the Union." Tucker points to Lincoln's own words which are frequently "omitted from the texts":

My paramount object in this struggle is to save the Union. . . If I could save the Union without freeing any slave I would do it, and if I could save it by freeing all the slaves I would do it; and if I could save it by freeing some and leaving others alone, I would also do that. What I do about slavery and the colored race, I do because I believe it helps to save this Union. . . .[15]

It is little wonder that the blacks, who are becoming increasingly educated about their past, desire recognition and full integration into American culture and history. Yet, for them the dream which was born in the 1960s is now dead. Tucker describes this in a chapter titled "The Death of a Movement" in his book *For Blacks Only* in which he writes, "The civil rights movement as such is dead. It is not just the singing and the marching that is over. The vast, organized, common effort to change the system, to erase the inequities has died away too."[16]

When one reads the history of the blacks in America, it is difficult to believe that "liberty and justice for all" was meant for anyone other than the white Anglo-Saxon Protestant. Such a glaring contradiction shows up the seamy side of America. This principle is true, to a lesser degree, for women.

Women: God Is Female

Women, in the history of America, have not necessarily been treated with violence in the fashion of Indians and blacks. Nevertheless, the left sees a kind of psychological violence perpetuated against them in the refusal to give them their proper place and role in society. Mary Beard in *America Through Women's Eyes* is hopeful that the new concern to write history from a sociological and integral approach will result in "disclosing woman's function and role in the clear light of research and understanding."[17]

It is a documented fact, as William L. O'Neill has shown in his work *The Woman Movement: Feminism in the United States and England,* that in America roles for women equivalent to men's roles have been resisted by a male-dominated society. In spite of this situation women have been able to make remarkable contributions to American life and culture.

There are reasons why women have played a significant part in American society. For one thing the presence of women on the frontier and their "legendary courage and fortitude gave the lie to those innumerable assumptions about women's inferior physiology and nervous system." Next, as women mobilized, especially in the church, through various charitable organizations and missionary societies, they discovered their own "talents and resources." These talents were further developed as women gained the right to be educated (Oberlin College was the first institution of higher learning in 1841 to admit women). These gains resulted in the tremendous energy poured into the women's movement of the 1830s and 40s. Women began making their mark on society only to receive a setback in the Victorian era when they were consciously forced into the mold of child rearing and the management of the home. In spite of several gains since that time women have yet to achieve their rightful place in American society, according to the left.

The issue of the current feminist movement was put succinctly by Dorothy Sayers in her work *Are Women Human?*:

"What," men have asked distractedly from the beginning of time, "what on earth do women want?" I do not know that women, as women, want anything in particular, but as human beings they want, my good men, exactly what you want yourselves: interesting occupation, reasonable freedom for their pleasures, and a sufficient emotional outlet.[19]

What women want is similarly defined in the *Official Report to the President, the Congress and the People of the United States* issued in 1977. In the *Declaration of American Women,* they protest that "man-made barriers, laws, social customs, and prejudices continue to keep a majority of women in an inferior position." Many women insist that their individuality, capabilities, and earning powers are diminished by discriminatory practices. They point out that they are "victims of crimes of violence in a culture that degrades us as sex objects and promotes pornography for profit." And they insist that they "lack effective political and economic power." They ask for "a full voice and role for women in determining the destiny of our world, our nation, our families, and our individual lives."[20]

These concerns are detailed by Kirsten Amundsen in *The Silenced Majority* where she sets out to demonstrate that women are still considered *inferior;* that women are *suppressed;* that women are *discriminated against;* and that women are *exploited.*[21]

For these reasons many women believe, as *The Declaration of American Women* states, that "only by bringing women into full partnership with men and respecting our

rights as half the human race can we hope to achieve a
world in which the whole human race—men, women, and
children—can live in peace and security."[22]

It is not surprising that the same note has been sounded
in the church as well. Christian feminists are demanding
that sexist language be taken out of the Bible and liturgy of
the church and that women be allowed the full rights of
ordination and other privileges hitherto given only to
males.

Criticism

Centrists are sympathetic to the Indian, the blacks, and
women and agree that their charges against the system of
oppression in the United States have considerable validity.
Therefore, the criticisms offered here are not against the
rights of minority groups. Rather, a question needs to be
raised about the assumption of the confluence of Marxism
and Christianity into a theology of liberation. Is it true that
"God is at work" in the history of liberating movements?

The above question is a point of great disagreement
among theologians. For the Moral Majority the assertion is
that God is at work in the American nation (although it
now needs to recover its original vision). For liberationists,
the assertion is that God is at work in history, and most
especially on the side of the poor and oppressed to accomplish their liberation. In general, this leads liberation
theologians to side with the economic system that is on the
"side of the poor." In America that system is generally seen
in socialism and the democratic platform. In other parts of
the world, especially the Third World, and among more
radical American church persons, the system in which God
is seen to be at work is Marxism.

Centrists reject the notion of "one history" and argue for
a "history within history"—namely, the notion that God is
on the side of the church, his divine institution, and not on
the side of any economic or political system (although it is

recognized that God is the Lord of all history). The church, however, is not unrelated to the history of the world. Consequently, the church has no excuse to be obscurantistic and to avoid the issue of the oppressed and the needy.

Because the church itself is the liberated society of God's people in this world, where reconciliation with God takes place, it must act as primary example of redeemed community. This, however, has not always been true of the church in American history. Sadly, we find that it has accommodated itself to the norms of society and participated in the oppression of Indians, blacks, women, and other minority groups.

Centrists believe that the church must be the major witness in voice and action agianst the evils of society. It must not, however, give wholehearted support to an agenda which arises out of a national economic or political system, lending it the right "God-words," reducing the radical salvation which is offered in Jesus Christ to a temporary relief from oppression. Otherwise the oppression will continue in another form.

Instead the church must act out its radical ethic by breaking with the oppressive norms of society and creating an example of that new society where unjust discrimination on the basis of race, color, and sex no longer exists. The sickness of the American church is not that it doesn't vote for a progressive economic and political system, but that it supports, protects, and passes down the discrimination, suppression, and injustices which are antithetical to the radical nature of a Christocentric ethic and a view of the church that Jesus is present to history in and through the church.

The answer to racism, prejudice, and oppression in this country lies with a repentant church—a church that will live out its calling to be a witness to and an instrument of the Kingdom. Consequently, centrists agree with the social concerns of the WCC (for the most part) but reject its commitment to fulfill the work of the church through any particular economic or social system. Centrists emphasize the role of the church as the community of the new humanity and advocate that believers find ways to mediate the ethics of the church through their vocational callings.

Chapter Seven

Liberation

In this chapter it will be argued that liberation ethics is the logical outcome of socialist economics coupled with a Marxist critique of society and an emphasis on the oppression of minority groups.

In order to understand the current liberation ethics of the left, we will look at the documents of the last meeting of the World Council of Churches in Nairobi (1975).[1] The two most important sections of the Nairobi report dealing with social issues are Section V, *Structures of Injustice and Struggles For Liberation,* and Section VI, *Human Development: Ambiguities of Power, Technology and Quality of Life.*

Structures of Injustice and Struggles for Liberation

The three major concerns treated under the above heading are human rights, sexism, and racism.

First, the Nairobi report correctly roots human rights in the doctrine that "all human beings are created in God's image." The result of this doctrine is that Christians ought to be led "into the struggle of the poor and the oppressed both within and outside the church as they seek to achieve their full human rights." What the report means by this is "that unjust social structures, expressed through economic exploitation, political manipulation, military power, class domination, and psychological conditioning, create the conditions under which human rights are denied." Therefore, the church is called to go beyond making *declarations* about human rights, to working for the full *implementation* of those rights."[2]

How the church is to work toward human rights is set forth in the following statement:

Local congregations should become more active in identifying, documenting, and combatting violations of human rights in their own communities. They and their national churches should seek ways to support the struggles of peoples, groups, and individuals for their own legitimate rights, helping them to form networks of solidarity to strengthen one another in their struggles.[3]

An essential feature of the WCC is that human rights are more important than property rights. This distinction was made clear in the Stockholm Conference of 1925 which called on Christians to "contend for the full and free development of the human personality" and insisted that industry "should not be based solely on the desire for individual profit, but that it should be conducted for the service of the community."[4]

Second, the concern about sexism is given serious attention at Nairobi. A statement calls for "the liberation of women from structures of injustice." The participants recognize that "as long as women are largely excluded from the decision making processes, they will be unable to realize a full partnership with men and therefore the church will be unable to realize its full unity."[5]

In order to accomplish these changes the committee recommended a thorough examination of "biblical and theological assumptions," paying particular attention to "the relationship of cultural assumptions and the way we understand the Word of God." Furthermore, it was recommended that the church's language about God should be more "inclusive," particularly its "liturgical language and practices."[6]

The third issue is racism. The articles on this subject reflect to some extent a sense of frustration and despair over the continuation and spread of racism. The statement condemns racism in no uncertain terms naming it "a sin against God," a practice "contrary to the justice and love of God revealed in Jesus Christ." It "destroys human dignity," "denies the very faith we express," and "undoes the credibility of the church."[7]

Recognizing that racism can be seen in every part of the world, the statement acknowledges that "racially oppressed communities are rapidly becoming aware of the injustices to which they are subjected and that they more and more refuse to endure indignity and exploitation. Consequently, they are increasingly determined to liberate themselves and thereby affirm their humanity." To this statement the committee adds, "we need to express our solidarity with them."[8]

Unfortunately racism is still found in the church, especially among those who "often reflect the racially prejudiced attitudes of their governments, their elites, and self-pretensions, while presuming that their own attitudes arise out of the Christian faith." Furthermore, there is still a considerable amount of institutional racism which is "imbedded in institutional structures that reinforce and perpetuate themselves, generally to the great advantage of the few and the disadvantage of many."[9]

For these reasons the Nairobi statement recommends that churches "ought to re-examine their use of human and material resources so that they can effectively support liberation efforts and contribute to human dignity in developing countries in ways that are beyond the scope of traditional patterns of giving and receiving."[10]

Human Development: Ambiguities of Power, Technology, and Quality of Life

In this section the articles of the World Council of

Churches deal with three issues: social responsibility in a technological age; towards acknowledgment of power; and quality of life.

First, social responsibility in a technological age recognizes that:

The world is on a catastrophic course leading to mass starvation, global depletion of resources, and global environmental deterioration. The responsibility that now confronts humanity is to make a deliberate transition to a sustainable global society in which science and technology will be mobilized to meet the basic physical and spiritual needs of people, to minimize human suffering, and to create an environment which can sustain a decent quality of life for all people. This will involve a radical transformation of civilization, new technologies, new uses for technology, and new global economic and political systems.[11]

In view of the current critical crisis of the world, the committee recommends energy conservation, discussion of the pro and cons of nuclear energy, an increased attention to alternative sources of energy, and a willingness to challenge the fact that "a large proportion of the world's wealth and scientific and technical manpower goes into weapons and military technology."[12]

Further, the report calls for "a fairer distribution of oil and mineral resources," the establishment of "an emergency food program," assistance to developing countries "for essential human needs, including food and energy." In addition, the report recognizes the "sanctity of human life and calls on the church to speak to the ethical issues created by abortion, euthanasia, genetic manipulation, and behavioral control."[13]

The second problem is that of power. Development not only has to do with economics, but with power structures which control the economic situation of a country. There are, of course, a number of different kinds of power. One kind is economic power which seeks to control the re-

sources of the world. Frequently economic power estab-
lishes "exploitive structures of domination and
dependence."[14] Colonialism is one example, transnational
corporations is another. Political power is another means of
control. Frequently political power becomes totalitarian,
using torture and terror as a means of maintaining control.
There are other kinds of power, some of which are less
obvious. Ideological power, for example, seeks control
through the mass media or education; military power
maintains zones of influence; "people's power" is grass
roots organization whose purpose is to struggle against the
dominating power.

What is the role of the church in the face of all these
powers? According to the Nairobi documents the church
"cannot speak about nor work for a new world order in the
midst of situations of domination and structures of oppression without referring to the liberating power of Jesus
Christ." Jesus is our liberator. He gives us hope and calls us
to overcome "the ambiguities of power" through love and
the way of the cross. For that reason it is "impossible to
ignore" the "role and the power" of the church in any
given concrete situation. The church is always engaged in
one way or another with the power structure; sometimes it
is in sympathy with the power structure, and sometimes it
is against the power structure. [15]

Whatever the situation, the church "cannot ignore
through [its] whole history . . . the existence of committed
people and churches for whom to be faithful to Jesus Christ
has implied and still implies to share with the oppressed
their struggles for liberation. The participation of the
Christian community in the struggle against poverty and
oppression is a sign of the answer to the call of Jesus Christ
to liberation."[16]

The third issue is the quality of life, which is related to all
the above issues. The problem is that technology has "de-
personalized and functionalized" many people. In this con-

dition people have been "alienated from our neighbor, nature, cosmos, and God." For this reason it is important to "assert our autonomy and control over the machines we have created—we must make them instruments not master."[17] This attitude should lead us to a rejection of "consumerism" and "giantism" and a commitment to help people meet the basic needs of "food, clothing, and medical care." To meet this need Christians are called to a "proper asceticism,"[18] a willingness to recognize that the "quality of life does not consist in the abundance of *more having* but in our *being* in relationship with the Father and with our brothers and sisters." For this reason the church calls on the affluent to recognize their obligation to "provide basic necessities for all the people of the planet earth, and to modify their own consumption patterns."[19]

Criticism

There is much within the World Council of Churches and its National American affiliate with which the centrist agrees. Certainly the centrist is supportive of human rights, rejects unjust discrimination on the basis of sex, and supports racial equality. Centrists are equally desirous to confront the powers, face the multifaceted issues of technology, and improve the quality of life. Nevertheless, centrists have three concerns with the program of the World Council of Churches.

First, there is a notable lack of involvement in the moral issues that touch personal and family life. Centrists perceive the WCC as wishy washy on abortion, permissive in sexual matters, open-ended regarding divorce, quiet regarding pornography, and lenient with regard to sexual improprieties on television and in the movies. This leads one to think that Christianity has much to do with the world issues of war and peace, economics and distribution of wealth, energy and environmental problems, but little to do with matters of personal morality and the witness to biblical values of the family and sexuality.

Second, the theme of liberation is not adequately rooted in the biblical Christ and the liberation from sin through faith in his death and resurrection. One is left with the impression that these are only symbols of revolution which can be applied indiscriminately to the emergence of any group from their oppression. Does this mean that the Christian religion is nothing more than a "mythological story" which provides a vision for the liberation of history from all forms of prejudice? Are traditional sexual taboos part of the prejudices from which we are to be liberated? Is the fight for the pro-gay movement a sign of God's liberating presence?

Third, the WCC does not have an adequate view of the church as that distinct supernatural society to which the redeemed give their earthly allegiance. The church takes a back seat to God's work in the political order—particularly in socialism or Marxism where the people are in the process of being freed from a totalitarian government. Consequently, *we find that not only the Moral Majority but also the WCC supports a kind of "civil religion"—one which takes economic and political sides, saying "that's where God is."* The fact that they support a *different* civil religion is less significant than the fact that they both support one *at all*. In turn the church suffers. Its identity as the radical society of God's people in an otherwise fallen world is blurred and its power to mediate the values of the Kingdom and its eschatological hope in the final victory of Christ are compromised for a local and temporary program of immediate justice which soon becomes a terror in its own right, even to the people who supported it.

Centrists are unwilling to make any holy alliances with the power structures of the world because they dilute the church and in the end become the enemy of the cross.

Consequently, the church loses its power to act as a social critic and to invite people into its own society which is called to be the only living alternative to the social order. Thus, the church is rendered ineffective in the world and becomes a bland supporter of the status quo.

Part III

Movement Toward the Center: Evangelical Centrists

Chapter Eight

World View

The térm centrist has been used frequently in the previous chapters. The remaining chapters of this book will deal more specifically with a definition of the centrists and a clarification of their viewpoint in contrast to the right and the left. We shall begin by affirming that centrists are represented by an evangelical viewpoint which has broadened considerably since the early 1970s.

Influences on an Evangelical Centrist Ideology
Reference has already been made to the relationship between fundamentalism and contemporary evangelicals. In a sense evangelicalism of the twentieth century may be regarded as an offspring of fundamentalism. However, it is an offspring much broader and more inclusive than its fundamentalist parent. The next few pages outline how this broadening has occurred and present the case for a more inclusive definition of contemporary evangelicalism.

After World War II a young group of fundamentalist-evangelical leaders were determined to overcome the negative image of fundamentalism and get back into the mainstream of issues.

These men, trained at some of the best universities, were intellectuals "aware of their times." Most of them. like Carl

F. H. Henry, E. J. Carnell, and Harold Lindsell, were Wheaton College graduates and contemporaries of Billy Graham. The sweeping success of Billy Graham and the financial backing of this group put these men and others in a position where they could form new organizations to communicate their agenda.

The principal platform of the new evangelical movement was enunciated by Harold Ockenga, pastor of Park Street Church in Boston. He called on fundamentalism to accomplish three goals: (1) restore social concern; (2) establish an intellectual defense and presentation of the gospel; and (3) enter into dialogue with mainstream liberal Christianity.

The new evangelicals founded Fuller Seminary in 1947 as their intellectual center and *Christianity Today* as their major literary organ. In the succeeding years literally hundreds of other media organizations, mission works, schools, and other agencies were formed.

With the revolution of the 1960s came the demise of liberal social programs and the emergence of a second wave of evangelical scholars, leaders, and social workers who wanted to carry the program laid out by the fathers of the new evangelical movement even further. Their concerns were to go beyond an individualistic Christianity and restore a faith which spoke to the public sector of life as well.

This stage of evangelicalism, which began in the seventies, has been expressed in four strategic documents and influenced by three different theological traditions.

The first of these centrist documents is *The Chicago Declaration* of 1973 which had as its major purpose the call to Christian social action. The second, *The Lausanne Covenant* of 1974, called evangelicals to a more inclusive understanding of evangelism. Evangelism was defined, not only in personal terms, but also, and more especially, in relationship to the public responsibility and accountability of the church. The third document was *The Chicago Call* of 1977 which was a call to churchmanship. The overriding concern of this document was to call evangelicals back to their historical roots and to a deeper, more comprehensive theology which reflects consistency with Orthodox and Catholic Christianity as defined by the early church fathers. The fourth document, *An Evangelical Commitment to Simple Lifestyle,* was written in 1980 by members of the World Evangelical Fellowship. This document calls evangelical Christians into a personal commitment to a simple lifestyle as an expression of faith and an act of love. (All these documents are contained in the appendixes.)

Three somewhat incongruous and seemingly incompatible theological and ecclesiastical traditions have influenced centrists: the catholic (or early church), the Anabaptist, and the Reformed traditions. In spite of their differences, these three views are giving shape to that large body of evangelicals called centrists.

In the first place the influence of the early church is bringing about a renewal of classical Christian theology. The special feature of this theology is its integral, dynamic, and holistic perspective. It brings together the major themes of Christian teaching such as creation, fall, revelation, incarnation, death, resurrection, and consummation into a single coherent whole. Consequently, centrists are moving away from a static propositional approach to theology toward a theological vision which sees life whole.

Strangely, the spiritual father of this movement in America is the literary don of Oxford, C. S. Lewis, and his larger circle of literary friends and forebears—George MacDonald, G. K. Chesterton, Charles Williams, J. R. R. Tolkien, Dorothy L. Sayers, and Owen Barfield. (The worldwide center for the study of this literature is in The Wade Collection at Wheaton College.) These writers were steeped in the writings of the early church fathers. Thus, through their literary works, the notions about the world and salvation as understood in classical Christianity is being indirectly spread. In addition, there is a renewed interest in patristics among evangelical theologians.

A second influence on evangelical centrists comes from

the Anabaptist quarter. Two special Anabaptist emphases are making an impact on evangelical centrists: lifestyle and social concern. The most influential translator of the classic vision of the Anabaptist to *live out* the Christian faith is John Howard Yoder. His book *The Politics of Jesus* is widely read and studied by evangelical scholars and students concerned about social ethics.

Anabaptist influences have also played a key part in developing Christian communities like Reba Place Fellowship in Evanston, Illinois. Furthermore, their books on community (e.g., Dave and Neta Jackson, *Coming Together*) have given practical instruction on community lifestyle and have helped evangelicals recover the church as the body of Christ.

The Anabaptist impact is seen particularly in what may be called the "left side" of the centrist spectrum, although it is broader than that in its general influence. Journals and the associated communities of the *Sojourners* and *The Other Side,* as well as the writings of Ron Sider, especially his best-selling book *Rich Christians in an Age of Hunger,* are good examples of the Anabaptist influence.

The third influential group among centrists are the Reformed Christians. The central feature of their influence is the concern to apply the Christian faith to all areas of life.

The most powerful translation of these ideas into the neo-evangelical community have come from the writings and lectures of Francis Schaeffer and Arthur Holmes.

Schaeffer has led the way toward a recovery of the relationship between theology and culture. His initial works *Escape From Reason* and *The God Who Is There* made a powerful impact on evangelicals, awakening them to cultural responsibility and sensitivity to the world around them.

Holmes' work has mainly been in the area of translating a Reformed world view consciousness into the evangelical community. His recent works on *The Idea of a Christian*

College and *All Truth Is God's Truth* have sensitized evangelicals to the religious nature of all life and work and have helped evangelicals break away from the privatization of faith which relegated God to personal experience.

In the area of political action, the Reformed community has inspired the most thoughtful work on the Christian in politics. Books such as Linder and Pierard, *Politics: A Case For Christian Action;* Paul Henry, *Politics For Evangelicals;* and Richard Mouw, *Politics and the Biblical Drama* and *Political Evangelism* have provoked thoughtful analysis of political action from an evangelical viewpoint.

Obviously, such an array of thinkers creates a diversity of opinion. Nevertheless, there is a remarkable consensus on basic issues among evangelical centrists.

From an ideological point of view evangelical centrists are honestly trying to deal with the biblical-theological-historical data that gives shape to a Christian mind and informs social action. For this reason evangelical centrists are not aligned with any one political party or economic system. Though this diversity sometimes leads to confusion, it almost always brings about dialogue and often creative insights. Therein lies the strength of evangelical centrism—its ability to draw upon and creatively use the best insights from a variety of Christian traditions.

Thus, the future of American Christianity does not appear to lie in the extreme left or right. Rather, there is movement from every quarter of the Christian church toward the center, toward an inclusive evangelicalism.

A Christian World View
A major disagreement centrists have with both the right and the left is with their approach to social action. There is a strong movement among centrists to return to what the ancient Catholics termed a "sacramental vision of life" or what the Reformers call a "world view." That is, centrists believe social action needs to be understood in terms of a

theology that draws on the biblical message in its entirety, beginning at creation and reaching fulfillment at consummation. This vision may be summarized in six themes: creation, the fall, revelation, the Christ-event, the church, and the consummation.[1]

First, for centrists the real significance of creation is not scientific, but religious. The emphasis is not when or how God created as much as it is one of meaning; i.e., because God created the world, the entire creation is endowed with meaning and significance. The idea that God created the world, then, carries with it several important notions: (1) it affirms that all creation is good, denying all gnostic, Manichaean, or contemporary rejections of the physical; (2) it affirms that the religious life is not fulfilled outside of creation, but rather within it and through it; and (3) it insists that all of life for the Christian is understood from a Christian viewpoint and that a Christian's vocation in the world is characterized by Christ-centered meaning.

For centrists the doctrine of creation means that we are made in the image of God, we "bear God's image." This confession speaks not only to the dignity of persons, but also to the task which people have in creation. The task is what is frequently called the "cultural mandate"—the calling to have "dominion," to "subdue" the earth, and "to till it and keep it." This means to unearth its treasures, to unfold its character, and to be God's steward of the earth and its resources.

The second conviction of the centrists is that humanity is fallen. The doctrine of the fall not only accounts for the origins of evil in the world, but also explains the origins of the satanic "powers" which seek to destroy persons and the creation. These satanic powers have unleashed a demonic and destructive force within creation which leads people and nations to a narcissistic self-interest, and generally, except for God's common grace, thwarts the purposes God meant for his image-bearers to fulfill on earth. Furthermore, centrists believe that the unfolding of culture throughout history reveals a commitment to the powers of evil. Thus, no society or nation has or ever will represent the Kingdom of God on earth.

Third, centrists believe in a supernatural revelation from God. God has not left his creatures to chance, nor to the development of their own set of standards. Rather, from the very beginning God has chosen a people through whom he has been especially involved in the history of the world. He has given to these people a special revelation of himself and of his will for them. In the Old Testament he gave the law (the Ten Commandments) to the people of Israel. These commands not only formed the basis of Israel's civil government and corporate life, but are equally important to the whole world, for they reveal how God made persons to live in harmony with himself and each other. These commands are not restrictions as much as they are guides to peace.

Fourth, the law, however, is not enough to save the world, for the world has to be freed from the power of sin, death, and the dominion of the devil. Only God himself can do that. Consequently, centrists confess Christ's incarnation, death, and resurrection as the crucial event in history which signals the final defeat of evil in the world, to be completed by the second coming of Christ, the consummation of history.

In order to save the creation, God became the creation and saved it in the body of his own creation. In the incarnation, through the womb of the Virgin Mary, God the creator received his own creation. In this human flesh God, the creator, lived in his own creation, taking into himself the sin and alienation of the creation. In this "body of death" Jesus was unjustly crucified and put to death. Although this seemed to be a victory for evil, it was in fact the victory of God. For God in Christ destroyed the power of death over his creation in the death of Christ. On the cross Christ, as Paul tells us, "disarmed the principalities and powers making a public example of them" (Col. 2:15).

In the resurrection Jesus demonstrated his power over death by being raised to life. This showed God's creative activity not only in the new body of Christ, but also in the potential re-creation of his entire creation (Rom. 8:18-25). Consequently, the centrist believes that sin has been conquered and that the hope of persons and the entire creation lies in the action of God in Christ to destroy evil—a hope which will be fully realized in the consummation.

Fifth, the church finds itself in the tension between the now (the defeat of evil on the cross) and the not yet (evil has not been completely eradicated from persons and the creation). Because the church is "the body of Christ" it cannot be regarded as a "collection of individuals." Centrists are rediscovering the church as the corporate body of Christ, the means through which Jesus himself is actually present to and in the world. The church, in mystical union with Jesus Christ its head, is called, therefore, to act in behalf of Christ, to do Christ's work in the world. Thus evil in all its forms—personal or public immorality, injustice, oppression, exploitation—must be attacked with the same vigor Jesus himself used when he attacked the evil of his day. Jesus Christ is the ultimate point of reference for Christians and their life in the world.

Sixth, the church as the extension of Christ's "body" in the world continues the cosmic struggle with evil. Because Jesus has in fact defeated the powers of evil on the cross the church receives his resurrection power by the Holy Spirit and is the focus of his continuing work in the world. Therefore, the church is called to claim the power of Christ's resurrection in its struggle against evil, living in the hope of the ultimate and final destruction of all evil in the consummation. In this way the church is a witness to the values of the kingdom and provides a continuing example of the presence of Jesus in the world. Thus, the role of the church in society is grounded in Christ and represents Christ to the social order.

Conclusion

The recovery of a world view by evangelical centrists is significant for several reasons. First, it signifies that evangelicals are moving from a static to a more dynamic conception of life. Centrists believe that a Christian world view gives the proper meaning to life from creation to consummation.

Second, a Christian world view provides the context in which centrists can develop a social ethic and public philosophy. This enables them to work toward the redemption of humanity in the midst of evil powers seeking to thwart it.

Third, a Christian world view focuses on Christ and his church. Consequently, centrists are increasingly aware of the church as the unique society of God's people in history, characterized by a call to extend his redemptive work in the life of the world.

How does this world view affect the centrists' interpretation of the role of the church in American society? It will become clear that the centrists do not view America as a "nation raised up by God" as do many people on the right. Nor do centrists regard America as "one of the most evil nations on earth" as do some extremists from the left. Rather, centrists recognize that the church in American society has gone through a number of different phases—sometimes misunderstood by society, sometimes challenging the evils of society, and other times accommodating itself to societal norms.

Chapter Nine

Civil Religion

A second area in which centrists take strong issue with both the right and the left is in their interpretation of America. A centrist rejects the "chosen nation" idea of the right and believes that the left's *preoccupation* with minority group history presents a distorted view of America (although centrists support increased attention to minority history and concerns).

A centrist calls for an intelligent, objective, and critical understanding of the relationship between the church and society in the American experience.[1] Centrists see a constant and changing interface between church and state in the entire history of America. They believe American Christians desperately need an objective understanding of that history to help them focus in a thoughtful way on the current face-off between church and state. This chapter provides a brief overview of the centrist interpretation of church and state in America, demonstrating that this country has been dominated by civil religion, the type of religion which the Moral Majority advocates today.

The Origin of the "America Is a Chosen Nation" Theme

The notion that America is a nation of God's chosen people

originated in the Puritan experience. It made such an impact on the American self-consciousness that it still exists today and can be found within both the church and the state. Several characteristics of the Puritans laid the basis for an American civil religion.

First, the Puritans were characterized by an intense conviction that God had selected them for a divine destiny in the New World. For this reason the theme that crossing the Atlantic was an exodus for God's "New English Israel" is predominant in many of the early sermons of Massachusetts. John Cotton even preached that New England was playing a major role in overthrowing anti-Christ and introducing the millennium. Thus the state became a "desired partner of the gospel." From this viewpoint William Penn attempted to establish a "holy experiment" (Pennsylvania) where "men of various religious and national backgrounds together could build a community of brotherly love." This gave "rise to feelings that God had chosen America as a special religious haven, a refuge in which the gospel could flourish."[2]

Second, the Puritans exalted the Old Testament model of church and society in which the state is seen as distinctly Christian. For example, the *New England Primer,* which taught children how to read, was filled with Bible stories; Harvard College students were admonished "to lay Christ in the bottom, as the only foundation of all knowledge and learning."[3] It must be remembered, however, by those who look to this period as a "golden era," that the Puritans did not believe in the separation of church and state and practiced a corporate and hierarchic view of society within which there was no freedom of dissent. Their social attitude was summed up in the motto, *salus populi suprema lex*—"the welfare of the people is the supreme law." This notion was expressed in the word "commonwealth" which obviously accented "the welfare of the whole, the well-being of all of society together." This viewpoint was based on the biblical idea that each individual must take "responsibility for the needs of his neighbor." Consequently, the amassing of private wealth and large estates was looked upon unfavorably.[4]

This sense of a "body politic" led them to deny the equality of all persons in society. This inequality was thought to apply more to the unequal importance of functions within society than to the intrinsic value of persons. Everyone had been placed in a particular place in society by God, and each had a particular calling. Governor Winthrop declared, "God Almighty in his most holy and wise providence hath so disposed of the conditions of mankind, as in all times some must be rich, some poor, some high and eminent in power and dignity, others mean and in subjection."[5] They shared these views with the typical European at that time.

But this whole notion of a corporate society was challenged by Roger Williams and others who advocated the separation of church and state and the freedom of conscience. This revolutionary change was based on the rise of Enlightenment ideas, especially individualism. Its result in American Christianity was to accent the notion that God was at work through the nation.

Further Development of the "Chosen Nation" Theme

The emergence of American individualism fanned by Enlightenment philosophy changed the American political, economic, and ecclesiastical practice 180 degrees from the original Puritan vision.

First, individualism challenged and broke down the corporate notion of society. Alexis de Tocqueville, who coined the word "individualism," described the Americans as "free, masterless individuals" who "sought absolute independence and equality of status." He said, "They imagine that their whole destiny is in their own hands."[6] This spirit of individualism affected American politics by foster-ing an "age when democracy first became the supreme political virtue. Any man's vote was as good as his neigh-bor's."[7] Individualism also changed the economic structure of America. Until this time the government controlled eco-nomics, but now the ideas of Adam Smith and *laissez faire* which insisted on the right of each individual to pursue his own interests became predominant. The assumption was that "as each atom in society went its own way, somehow the good of the whole would be met."[8]

Second, the emphasis on individualism had two signifi-cant effects on the church. In the first place, it resulted in the anti-historical attitude which is commonplace in Amer-ican evangelicalism. The past experience of the church, par-ticularly that of the fathers and even the Reformers, became increasingly irrelevant, gradually being replaced by the ex-perience of the individual. Secondly, it undermined the au-thority of local church officers. It was now accepted by increasing numbers of Christians that a "converted man guided by the Holy Spirit needed no guidance from theolog-ically trained clergymen, no supervision from ecclesiasti-cal authorities."[9]

Consequently, individualism led to the decreasing im-portance of the church as a divine institution. Christian faith became personal and private and the church became a mere "voluntary association" of individual believers.

The rise of individualism had both positive and negative effects. On the positive side it stressed the necessity of per-sonal faith and piety. The negative effect showed up in the inability of the church as a corporate body to make an impact on institutional evil. Thus the church retreated from social reform in the public arena into the private personal life of the individual.[10]

This shift from corporate to private resulted in two dis-tinct changes in the relationship between the church and the state. First, evangelical pulpits and congregations "generally ceased to deal seriously with social issues. Ministers no longer concentrated on relating the gospel to political and economic decisions that laymen had to make."[11] Second, Christians became convinced that *the primary agent through which God works in history was not the church but the nation.* Thus America was given a religious purpose in the world. Evangelist Lyman Beecher expressed this well: "only America can provide the physical effort and moral power to evangelize the world."[12] The new contours of an American civil religion were beginning to take shape. The idea that the nation and not the church was the focus of God's activity in America was to play a formative role in creating a misguided American Messianic complex.

The Emergence of American Civil Religion

Because the nation now had a new religious purpose, the groundwork had been laid to see the American Revolution as a theological event. The Revolution and the subsequent Declaration of Independence were cast in a strong religious context. "The convictions that men had rights by nature, that the pursuit of personal happiness was an inalienable right, that all men were essentially equal, and that personal freedom was necessary for societal well-being influenced the thinking of the American church fathers as well as the founding fathers."[13] Therefore, the Revolution could be seen as God-ordained and God-glorifying.

In the second place, the Revolution fed into the growing concern to keep church and state separate. British meddling in colonial affairs produced strong resentment against governmental interference in personal life. The rise of individualism had already reshaped the conception of most Americans toward a voluntaristic church. The natural consequence of these two trends was to keep government and the church in the separate spheres of jurisdiction where they belong.[14]

Finally, the Revolution cemented the notion that this was

indeed God's nation, and the "holy calling" of America became widely accepted. This attitude fostered the notion that America was elect because "of the heights of civil liberty that it had achieved." Here is the foundation of civil religion, for it "allowed men to express secular purposes in religious terms." Consequently, it was believed that the expansion of a republican form of government would accompany the spread of the gospel. Some Christians persisted in interpreting the Revolution as the emergence of a Christian society. In this context "ministers became high priests of the new republic" and were, therefore, "less able to serve as prophets" to the national consciousness. Unfortunately, despite the notion that church and state were to be kept separate, the church unwittingly provided religious support for national policies; an American civil religion had been born.[15]

Nineteenth-century Evangelicalism and American Civil Religion

The relationship between evangelicals and the nation was so strong after the Revolution that historians have named the early 1800s as the period of an "Evangelical Empire." Evangelicalism became a kind of national religion. It was so pervasive that Alexis de Tocqueville noted that "no country in the whole world existed in which the Christian religion retains a greater influence over the souls of men than in America."[16]

These evangelicals set as their goal the Christianizing of America, seeking not only to evangelize people, but to purge all forms of social evil. Through the revivals of Charles G. Finney, evangelicals were motivated toward involvement in all manner of social reform. Evangelicals were leaders in "anti-slavery, temperance, women's rights, education, poor relief, and prison and hospital reform."[17]

In spite of these accomplishments evangelicals were characterized by several blind spots. For one, as evangelicals increasingly shaped the values of society, it became more difficult to distinguish between the Kingdom of God and the republic. Like Constantinianism, Americans lost the sharp distinction between civil goodness and the church as the society of the age to come. Consequently, missionary expansion was as much an extension of Americanism as a concern to preach the gospel. Furthermore, their intolerance of those who disagreed with them, particularly the Catholics, gave a legalistic shape to their religion. And finally, the failure of most evangelicals to oppose the institution of slavery suggests they were, at that point especially, unable to extricate themselves from a national consciousness to assume a prophetic role. The same is true today, and always will be when the churches compromise their message of regeneration in exchange for civil religion.

Critique

How do the centrists view the past development of the American civil religion and what does the centrist have to say about the present resurgence of civil religion in the Moral Majority? Centrists regard the development of American civil religion as a mistake and do not support its current resurgence in the Moral Majority. There are two reasons for this stance.

First, God has no interest in religion *per se*. Civil religion fosters a religious veneer, a comfortable use of "God-words," an outward show of piety. While no centrist would advocate the neglect of the moral and spiritual influence of the church in the American society, centrists recognize that a religious renewal that is *distinctly Christian* is the only answer that deals with the real issue. The idea that all people of high principle should unite to recover America's moral heritage is a moralism that feeds into civil religion. It is not a distinctly Christian message that demands regeneration into Jesus Christ and absolute obedience to the moral precepts given by him to the church. The church does not advocate moralism so much as it calls men and women into a radical transformation of character through faith in Jesus Christ and obedience to his teaching. Moral reform is the *by-product* of this change, not its goal. True moral reform comes as the result of faith in Jesus Christ, not from the desire to create "national solidarity and stability."

Second, God judges people not by outward conformity, but by the heart. Thus in seeking to mediate its values to society the church must invite people to faith in Jesus Christ as the source of true values. This does not mean that the church can settle for mass evangelism and feel its job is done. Rather, as Christians pursue many vocations in a social order that is "under the powers," they must make clear that values are not self-evident but arise from revelation, exemplified in Jesus Christ and preserved in the church. The absolute nature of these values cannot be compromised. In some cases this may mean confronting the powers, even if that confrontation entails the loss of a vocation and the ridicule of fellow workers. In this way the adoption and living out of Christian values become a witness to Christ, an invitation to "take up the cross, and follow him."

The most powerful weapon the evangelical church has against the breakdown of morals in our culture is not the restoration of a civil religion. It is rather the preaching of Jesus Christ as Lord, the invitation for people to join with Christ's church, and a renewed understanding of the church as the universal society of God's people called to live in obedience to Jesus Christ's teachings.

This, coupled with the emergence of a church that lives out the existence of Jesus in the world, is the way to make a lasting impact on this country and the world. This course of action has far more potential than a mere return to a civil religion that compromises the church and makes it the source of religious sanction to such questionable national policies as military buildup, restriction of liberties, and morality by coercion.

Chapter Ten

Private and Public Ethics

A third area in which evangelical centrists disagree with both the right and the left is in the issues they choose to tackle. The right tends to emphasize personal moral issues (although this is changing) and the left tends to emphasize socio-economic issues (this may also change due to the impact of the Moral Majority). On the other hand, centrists are committed to both personal and social ethics and encourage any movement in that direction by both the right and the left.

Because centrists are concerned with both personal and public issues they find themselves in the unusual position of affirming many of the stands taken by both the Moral Majority and the WCC. Nevertheless, because centrists approach these issues from a biblical world view rather than a particular economic or political bias, there is a fundamental difference in tactics and purpose. In the next chapter these differences will be discussed. The purpose of this chapter is to provide evidence of the union of personal and public ethics and to briefly state the viewpoint of the centrists.

The centrists' concern to bring the personal and public ethic together is prominently stated in their recent public documents. For example, *The Chicago Declaration* includes the following words in the opening paragraph: "We affirm that God lays total claim upon the lives of His people. We cannot, therefore, separate our lives in Christ from the situation in which God has placed us in the United States and the world." In *The Lausanne Covenant* it is put this way: "The results of evangelism include obedience to Christ, incorporation into his church and responsible service to the world." *The Chicago Call* sets forth the strongest statement: "We deplore the tendency of evangelicals to understand salvation solely as an individual, spiritual, and other-worldly matter to the neglect of the corporate, physical, and this-worldly implications of God's saving activity." Finally, the whole of *An Evangelical Commitment to Simple Lifestyle* weaves the personal and public Christian ethic into a consistent whole.[1]

At least eleven issues have received prominent attention by the centrists. What follows is a listing of these and a brief discussion of the centrist approach.

Personal Morality

Private and personal morality have stood at the center of evangelicalism from its very beginning. In some cases our personal ethics in the past have bordered on legalism—living according to a set pattern of rules as a means of attaining personal holiness. On the other hand, evangelicals have always taken a dim view of sexual promiscuity, including fornication, adultery, homosexual relationships, pornography, and personal habits such as excessive drinking and smoking and others which are damaging to the body. The point is that centrists find great sympathy with the moral concerns articulated by the Moral Majority and are alarmed by the ever-increasing spread of personal permissiveness and moral decadence of American society at large.

Pro-life

Evangelicals are united in their concern over abortion on demand. This irresponsible approach to life means a loss of human rights. Centrists challenge the reductionist view of life that says "all the marvels of creation are . . . mechanisms rather than mysteries." Evangelicals reject the mechanist's assertion that "the human brain is nothing more than an immensely complicated computer" and the conclusion that "it is no longer necessary to involve metaphysics to explain how it works." This outlook reduces human life to ultimate meaninglessness. As Francis Schaeffer says, "This view drastically reduces our view of self-worth as well as our estimation of the worth of others, for we are viewing ourselves as mere accidents of the universe."[2] Thus, pro-life issues extend to questions of genetic manipulation and bio-ethics in general, as well as abortion.

Pro-family

Evangelicals are also concerned for the preservation of the family. A number of local and national organizations are emerging to support the pro-family viewpoint as essential to the Christian church. These groups have organized local counseling clinics which are supported by a group of local churches and serve their constituency.

The family issue is increasingly recognized by evangelical seminaries and colleges. To meet this need courses and even majors are being introduced to help future pastors, leaders, and families prepare to understand and deal with the increasing pressures placed upon the family. For example, Fuller Seminary has introduced a two-year major in marriage and family ministries. In a recent issue of Fuller's periodical *Theology News and Notes,* Fuller reports several concerns for the future:

1. The church of the 1980s must develop a priority ministry to the family.
2. The church of the 1980s must address the issues of marriage, divorce, and singleness.

3. The home must be trained as the center of Christian education.

Centrists expect the family issue will grow considerably in the 1980s. They believe the current focus on the family by educators will result in increased knowledge and sophistication in matters dealing with the family.

Support for Justice

The writers of the *Lausanne Covenant* commend a "concern for justice and reconciliation throughout human society and for the liberation of men from every kind of oppression" and call on Christians to "stand against injustice and to remain faithful to the Gospel, whatever the cost." Centrists' documents recognize that an important feature of justice is an equitable use of the earth's resources. They flatly state that it is not fair for one-third of the world to consume two-thirds of the world's food and energy resources.

Centrists now acknowledge that a foundational problem is that Americans have accepted the Enlightenment opinion that science and technology would free humanity through material abundance and unlimited economic growth. This economic policy has not worked because the earth's resources are *finite*. Consequently, plundering the earth's resources for the benefit of one-third of its people has strengthened the patterns of injustice and will ultimately lead to increased conflict.

Some centrists are increasingly attracted to the alternative of a limited growth, steady state economy. To achieve this goal, however, we must establish a new value system and a new vision of human fulfillment. Political and economic power would have to be decentralized and diffused among the people. This would mean an alteration of personal and public lifestyle. Centrists do not believe the secular society is able to provide the leadership needed to attain this vision.

Rather, it must come from the Christian community. Thus, "Christians are faced with two challenges: to provide a new ethic of stewardship that can guide the direction of society; and to become the model of that vision."[3]

Concern for the Poor

To some extent evangelical Christians are already providing this model in their concern for the poor. Again, *The Lausanne Covenant* affirms that "evangelism and socio-political involvement are both part of our Christian duty . . . the message of reconciliation implies also a message of judgment upon every form of alienation, oppression and discrimination, and we should not be afraid to denounce evil and injustice wherever they exist."

One of the most visible demonstrations of evangelical concern for the poor has been the rise of evangelical communities. Most of these are in the inner-city. Many of their members have committed themselves to live at a poverty level in order to share their money and time with others in need.

Churches have also been drawn into support of the poor through cooperation with worldwide relief organizations, often extending into Third World countries. In November of 1978 ten evangelical relief groups formed an umbrellalike organization called the Association of Evangelical Relief and Development Organizations (AERDO). This group also spawned the Consortium of Evangelical Relief and Development Organizations (CERDO). The following description of the work of the ERDOs is taken from the report of President John Robinson.

All the ERDOs engage in functions related to development and/ or emergency relief primarily in the low-income countries. The type of development aid that the ERDOs intend to provide is not uniform. Some focus primarily on resource aid, the transfer of resources in cash and kind, in skilled manpower and technological know-how. The primary purpose of resource aid is to enable the recipients to improve their standard of living by providing for themselves better education, health, agriculture, and other social services within the existing economic and political structures. Other ERDOs are beginning to focus more attention on structural aid by attempting to modify existing economic and political structures in order to achieve greater justice, liberation from exploitation and humiliation.

Racism Rejected

Another area of concern is the continued presence of racism in America and around the world. Although *The Lausanne Covenant* contains no specific statement on racism, it condemns every form of "discrimination" and calls for liberation from "every kind of oppression."

More to the point is this statement in *The Chicago Declaration:*

We deplore the historical involvement of the church in America with racism and the conspicuous responsibility of the evangelical community for perpetuating the personal attitudes and institutional structures that have divided the body of Christ along color lines. Further, we have failed to condemn the exploitation of racism at home and abroad by our economic system.

While there has been improvement since 1973, centrists are in agreement that we still have a long way to go.

Materialism Rejected

Next, materialism is increasingly becoming a matter of concern to evangelicals. *The Chicago Declaration* speaks specifically to this matter in the following words:

We must attack the materialism of our culture and the maldistribution of the nation's wealth and services. We recognize that as a nation we play a crucial role in the imbalance and injustice of international trade and development. Before God and a billion hungry neighbors, we must rethink our values regarding our present standard of living and promote more just acquisition and distribution of the world's resources.

The centrist stand against the accumulation of wealth and the so-called "prosperity cult" is made more personal in *An Evangelical Commitment to Simple Lifestyle*. The authors call some "to follow him (Jesus) in a lifestyle of total, voluntary poverty" and insists that "all his followers" must be characterized by "an inner freedom from the seduction of riches." The authors call on Christians to re-examine their "income and expenditure, in order to manage on less and give away more." Both churches and para-church agencies are admonished "to be acutely aware of the need for integrity in corporate lifestyle and witness." In the decades ahead the church must move toward a simple lifestyle and lead the way in the rejection of a materialistic spirit.

Militarism Questioned
Another area which is receiving more attention from centrists is the issue of militarism. Although it is not mentioned by *The Lausanne Covenant*, it is singled out as an issue which cries for attention by *The Chicago Declaration*:

We acknowledge our Christian responsibilities of citizenship. Therefore, we must challenge the misplaced trust of the nation in economic and military might—a proud trust that promotes a national pathology of war and violence which victimizes our neighbors at home and abroad. We must resist the temptation to make the nation and its institutions objects of near-religious loyalty.

It would be a mistake to assume much uniformity on this issue among centrists. Centrists are unanimous in rejecting trust in military might. Nevertheless some argue for the reasonableness, even the moral necessity, of certain wars, while others argue for biblical pacifism and reject all killing as an option for Christians. An important feature of contemporary centrists is the growing numbers who call upon Christians to be pacifists. This represents a broadening of opinion from the time when most evangelicals gave whole-hearted support to the war in Viet Nam.

Human Rights Supported

Another issue for evangelicals is the matter of human rights. The writers of *The Lausanne Covenant* set forth their support of the Universal Declaration of Human Rights and express "deep concern for all who have been unjustly imprisoned, and especially for our brethren who are suffering for their testimony to the Lord Jesus Christ."

The increasing importance of human rights issues among evangelicals may be illustrated by a Wheaton College student-sponsored participation in a protest march in Chicago over the arrest of the Russian Orthodox priest Dimitri Dudko. Another example is the Slavic Gospel Association, an evangelical organization located in Wheaton, which has taken an active role in supporting religious dissidents in Soviet countries and offering financial help for their immigration. They have been directly involved in providing housing, jobs, education in English, and other necessities for those who have settled in the Chicago area. In this they have demonstrated not only their concern for human rights, but their expertise in applying the gospel to an issue of increasing social concern.

Sexism a Matter of Concern

Evangelicals have also been involved in the issue of sexism. *The Chicago Declaration* contains the following rather mild statement: "We acknowledge that we have encouraged men to prideful domination and women to irresponsible passivity. So we call both men and women to mutual submission and active discipleship."

Centrists are becoming increasingly aware of women's rights. Nevertheless, evangelicals will not support the radical side of feminism which puts down motherhood, advocates the breakdown of the heterosexual family, promotes homosexual marriages, and demands the rewriting of the Bible to "de-sex" its language. Centrists regard these viewpoints as inconsistent with the way God made us, and neglectful of normative male-female relationships. But centrists support women who want to have careers, believe in equal pay and opportunity, and advocate that husbands take a more active role in fathering their children.

Energy an Issue of Stewardship
Centrists take a keen interest in the matter of stewardship. The writers of *An Evangelical Commitment to Simple Lifestyle* recognize that "God's creation is marked by rich abundance and diversity, and he intends its resources to be husbanded and shared for the benefit of all." For this reason they denounce "environmental destruction, wastefulness and hoarding."

Centrists recognize the need for a harmonious relationship with the earth where persons "balance dominion with service." Centrists, however, do not reject the value of technology nor deny the importance of human values of equitable living. This concern for stewardship of the earth suggests that "we extend our awareness of the impact of our actions beyond our families, friends, and neighbors, to all peoples of the earth, to future generations, and to the whole household; the *oikouméne,* or ecosphere—all the interrelated life of the planet."[4]

Conclusion
This section has outlined some of the ways contemporary evangelical centricism stands between the right and the left. This does not mean that centrists have "arrived." But it does mean that they represent a maturing and balanced expression of the Christian faith in America and around the world in the area of social concern.

They have their feet firmly planted in a Christian world view, they have an intelligent and balanced view of the relationship between the church and state in American history, and they are increasingly seeking to speak to both private and public morality. For this reason evangelical centrism has the potential to provide insightful and positive leadership in the church and through Christians in various vocations who will increasingly confront the "powers" with a Christian ethic.

Part IV

The Prophetic Center:
A Biblical Agenda

Chapter Eleven

Differences

The purpose of this section is to set forth the centrist position regarding the church in the world more systematically. This chapter presents a summary of the major disagreements centrists have with the methodology of the right and the left. Chapter 12 sets forth a clear statement on the centrists' approach to social issues. The final chapter discusses four major issues which centrists believe must be tackled by Christians.

Differences with the Right

The major differences centrists have with the right and left are over foundational matters—those ideological frames of reference out of which their methods of social involvement derive. These are the grids through which their moral issues are filtered and enforced.

First, centrists do not agree that the free enterprise economic system is "biblical." To say as Jerry Falwell does that the free enterprise system is "clearly outlined" in Proverbs, or that Jesus was clear about the "work ethic," or that "competition in business is biblical" and that "ambitions and successful business management is clearly outlined as a part of God's plan for His people" is an example of how mistaken a well-intended person can be when he or she reads the Bible through the grid of a particular Western economic and political viewpoint.

The modern notion of the "free enterprise" system and of "competition" and "success" in business is rooted in the philosophy of the economist Adam Smith who applied the secular mechanistic world view to economics. Smith, a product of the Enlightenment, set forth his theory in 1776 in a book titled *An Inquiry Into the Nature and Cause of the Wealth of Nations.* In this work he discussed the relationship between freedom and order and analyzed the economic process to create a social theory. His major thesis is that human progress is only possible in a society where *individuals follow their self-interests.*

The point Smith makes is that when government takes a "hands-off" policy, individuals are free to produce things that others will buy. Buyers will buy what they need or want resulting in an economic pattern of producing and purchasing that balances out in the end. In this context a high value is placed on "work," "competition," and "success." The role of the government is to preserve law and order, enforce justice, defend the nation, and provide for the few social needs that cannot be met in the market.

Actually Adam Smith set forth a view of *conservative humanism* which believes in humanity's ability to create the good world. Smith failed to take into account the radical nature of evil and the effect it has had on people and cultural development. Nor did he account for human greed or mankind's proclivity toward self-interest that results in wealth, power, and control. Ironically, the philosophy of Smith as seen in the words of Thomas Jefferson that "the government that governs least, governs best" becomes the secular humanism which the Moral Majority so vehemently rejects. It is a viewpoint that believes in the basic goodness of humanity and argues for the creation of a better world built on the instincts and program of that goodness. Centrists feel that the Moral Majority has "baptized" and "Christianized" this economic and political secularism, reading it back into the Bible as though it is divinely inspired Truth.

Therefore, centrists cannot agree with the way the Moral Majority ties economics, politics, and moral issues together. To suggest that a basic reason this country is in a "moral mess" is rooted in a departure from a conservative economic and political viewpoint fails to properly understand the pervasive influence of evil, not only in persons but in the economic and political systems developed by persons.

Centrists believe that the free enterprise system and the political party based on the dictum of "least government" is subject to misuse and abuse because of the fallen nature of persons. Considering the abuses of capitalism and republicanism by sinful people, it is hard to believe that a mere return to these systems run by "Christians" or "moral people" is a road to morality and peace.

Unfortunately, the Moral Majority does not take the fall of humanity seriously enough to satisfy the centrists. Consequently, while they agree with many of the moral issues, they reject the assumption that American moral decadence is linked to the departure from free enterprise economics and the political stance it upholds.

The second objection centrists have with the right is the view that America is a special nation raised up by God for a specific mission to the world. Falwell believes that God promoted America to a greatness no other nation has ever enjoyed because her heritage is one of a republic governed by laws predicated on the Bible. This viewpoint leaves the impression that America was once a Christian nation, and that more recently it has fallen out of favor with God. Centrists disagree with this view of America.

An accurate reading of the origins of America certainly demonstrate a religious influence in the founding of this nation. But to suggest that our founding fathers were committed Christians is a strange and mistaken notion. While some of the founding fathers were genuine Christians, the great majority of them were committed to an "Enlightenment religion." It is true that their concern for individuals, for freedom, and for moral restraints reflected biblical principles. But these concerns were filtered through an Enlightenment grid.

For example, J. Bronoaski and Bruce Mazlish in *The Western Intellectual Tradition* tell how Ben Franklin opposed Thomas Jefferson's description of the fundamental principles of the Declaration of Independence as "sacred and undeniable." Franklin insisted on the word "self-evident" because he "did not want any principles, however ethical and religious they might be, to be received by sacred authority; he wanted ethics and religion to be accepted by the free acquiescence of the mind."[1] Franklin was giving expression to an Enlightenment viewpoint which rejected biblical revelation as the source of Truth. For him, truth is "self-evident." Thus, to suggest as the Moral Majority does that this nation was founded on a belief in the Bible is misleading. It is more correct to say that the founders of our country were in agreement with moral principles which they believed were derived from reason.

Centrists argue that the founding fathers' hope for America was not based on the Bible but on their conviction of the inherent goodness of humanity and in the ability of human beings to live according to "self-evident" truths. Centrists regard the belief that America was "raised up" as a Christian nation as a poor reading of the facts and an unwarranted elevation of the nation. This viewpoint has resulted in a near "Messianic trust" in the nation—a feeling that America is the Savior of the world.

The third disagreement centrists have with the Moral Majority lies in the area of tactics. An example of this is their "single issue" approach to evaluating the moral integrity of political candidates. For example, Republican Representative Robert E. Bauman received a high moral rating from the Moral Majority for originating a bill that would permit states to deny all Medicaid abortions and for sponsoring the family protection act which guaranteed employers the right to deny employment to "individuals who are homosexuals or proclaim homosexual tendencies."[2] Yet Bauman is a confessed alcoholic and recently admitted to soliciting sex from a sixteen-year-old boy. While some Moral Majority leaders condemned him for his personal practice, they continued to give him a high rating for his public stand. But these same persons would not apply similar logic to Senator Kennedy whose personal life is highly questionable, but who in his public office seeks moral legislation for blacks and the poor.

Furthermore, such a test puts a man like Senator Hatfield in an awkward position.[3] He is a man who as much as any Christian politician has sought to exercise a Christian conscience in politics. His personal life as well as his personal moral convictions are not taken into account because he has disagreed in good faith with the Moral Majority position on Salt II which they regard as "the Christian way."

Furthermore, this absolutizing of a political stance results in a tightly bound political and spiritual legalism. Since the Moral Majority so closely aligned with fundamentalism, they have made it difficult to separate spiritual commitment from economic and political commitment. Consequently, it has become increasingly easy to judge a person's spiritual stand by his or her political stand. For to affirm the "right" political stance must mean that everything else in one's house is in order. For example, the exuberance of the Rev. George Zorris of St. Charles, Illinois, over the results of the 1980 election expresses a political and spiritual legalism. Zorris, who organized his church to register and vote, claimed a ninety-nine percent turnout at the polls. His assistant Terry Crague said, "If anybody in our church was for Carter or Anderson, I don't know him." Furthermore, he went on to say, "I don't think they'd admit it." This is a kind of legalism rejected by centrists. Centrists reject this kind of partisanship in the church as a dangerous mixture of religion and politics which leads to spiritual stagnation and legalism.

Differences with the Left
The centrist disagreement with the left, like that of its disagreement with the right, is on the level of their ideology, their view of America, and the subsequent legalism which arises from these foundational commitments.

First, centrists believe the ideology of the World Council of Churches is as much a distortion of biblical principles as that of the Moral Majority. They take select passages of Scripture and read them through the grid of a Marxist critique and a socialist economic and political agenda. In this sense they are no less guilty of "politicizing" the gospel than the right.

Centrists believe that the social agenda of the left is rooted in the Enlightenment, particularly in the writings of Karl Marx. Marx, who held a mechanistic view of the world, set forth a viewpoint that reflects the Enlightenment faith in persons in a way different than that of Adam Smith. Marx interpreted history as a continual struggle between classes. This struggle, he believed, would one day end and humanity would live in peace with each other in a form of communism—the communal sharing of all goods.

Marx and his friend Friedrich Engels laid out the program for an achievement of the "golden era" in their famous work, *The Communist Manifesto*. In this work Marx and Engels perceived the *bourgeois* (capitalists) as having enslaved the *proletariat* (working men). They urged the proletariat to revolt and set up a planned economy in which the government would own all the property.

Recent theology, particularly *liberation theology,* has bought into the Marxist critique and now interprets much of Scripture (the Exodus for example) in light of the class struggle. Liberationists identify Jesus with all "liberation movements," particularly those movements which intend to free people from their oppressors.

While centrists acknowledge that the gospel does indeed liberate the poor and the oppressed, they are uncomfortable with the connections made by the left wing of the church with leftist political movements. These connections tend to politicize the gospel and make the church an accomplice in particularized social and cultural revolutions. In this way the church's role in the world is accommodated to social progress, and the distinction between social and economic revolution and the church as a prophetic voice within society becomes blurred. The result is an interpretation of history past, present, and future which is out of focus and a spiritual legalism no less lethal than that of the right.

This is true, for example, in the interpretation of America. The centrist agrees with the left with its sympathy for native Americans and blacks. Indeed, the centrist agrees that the "dark side" of America must be seen and that the treatment of minorities in America is a "moral problem."

But the centrists take issue with the support the left gives to violent revolution as a means of attaining rights for the underprivileged. This is not as acute a problem in America now as it has been or may be in the near future. It is a current problem, however, in those countries where the WCC has a record of supporting socio-economic-political revolution in the name of the gospel.

For example, the support of terrorist groups in Africa by the WCC has been a highly controversial matter even within the WCC. Since 1980 the WCC has given thousands of dollars to terrorist groups to engage in guerrilla warfare. WCC leaders have openly said that money has been given in support of the "just" terrorist causes. The issue here is not whether people have been oppressed and need to be liberated. The issue is whether church funds should be given in support of violent revolutions which are maneuvered by terrorists whose sympathies to the goals of communism are well known.

Centrists disagree not only with violent revolution and the political goals it represents, but more particularly with the naive utopianism it represents. At bottom, the WCC is giving support to an ideology that ultimately believes in the "goodness of humanity." Furthermore, it is supporting violence as a proper method to establish "goodness." This approach is not biblical enough for centrists because it denies the fallenness of humanity and places a messianic eschatalogical hope in "humanitarian" revolutions.

Finally, centrists see that the left is just as guilty of creating a spiritual legalism as the right. It is interesting to observe how angry the left is at the Moral Majority using the church to propagate their moral views. Vernon Royster in the *Wall Street Journal* takes the left to task for their blatant inconsistency in this matter. He chides liberals for citing fundamentalists as "a clear and present danger" and for arguing that "under the American system they have no right to judge others." "Religion," Royster says, "has been a part of American politics from the beginning. Pulpit voices played a role in making our revolution. They sounded loud and clear in their moral indignation at slavery and at those in politics who countenanced it. Their influence helped pass the 13th Amendment, which abolished it."[4]

The current anti-right movement headed by Norman Lear directly contradicts liberal "pulpit" and "political organization" politics of the sixties. Attempts by his group and by the American Civil Liberties Union to muzzle the Moral Majority are in absolute antithesis to the freedom of speech which they hold so dearly. Columnist James Hitchcock tellingly makes this point against Lear. In the *National Catholic Register,* Hitchcock calls Lear "an unabashed secular humanist with no love for religion." Hitchcock charges him with wanting "to protect the privileged position that secularism now has in our society."[5] Lear is annoyed that someone wants to present an alternate to his secular views promoted in *Maude* and *Mary Hartman, Mary Hartman*. Thus the liberal left is as legalistic as the right. For this reason, centrists would agree with the judgment of Methodist Alan Walker who told delegates to the 98th Methodist Conference of Southern Africa that "there is not much difference between the extreme left and the extreme right."

An Appeal to Move to the Center

The centrists' concerns about the right and the left are somewhat similar. Centrists argue first that both the right and left tend toward an alliance with a particular political party. Centrists do not believe a biblical case can be made for either capitalism or socialism. Therefore, centrists are unwilling to make "holy alliances" with particular economic and political systems. Rather, centrists insist that Christians are free to function in relation to all earthly systems, giving ultimate allegiance to none but the Kingdom of God.

Second, centrists believe both the right and the left are guilty of selecting only those issues that fit their ideology. While the Moral Majority has not given adequate active and visible support to programs for the poor and needy, the WCC has failed to speak out against or do anything to curb abortion, moral permissiveness in popular culture, and the proliferation of pornography. Centrists, on the other hand, are calling for a social involvement that brings together both the personal and the public ethic.

Third, centrists see legalism infecting both the right and the left. Legalism stifles true Christianity by creating an atmosphere of criticism, intolerance, and bigotry. According to centrists this legalism of the left and right is the product of ideology. Centrists try to avoid becoming ideological. For this reason they are less utopian about their ideas and more apt to work quietly without fanfare in a variety of ways and in many different levels of social structures and influence.

The fourth problem centrists have with the right and the

left is that they seem to lack love toward each other. Certainly love is a cardinal teaching of the Christian church. Whenever we fail to love each other we make a mockery of the Christian faith and present a lie to the world we are seeking to win for Jesus Christ.

It may be utopian to hold out the ideal for the right and the left to come to the center. The church has almost always existed with tensions to the right and left, with a large group in the middle. The value of these differences, when they are held in love, is that the church thinks and acts more carefully. But when the church is torn by differences, and acts without love and understanding, its work in the world suffers. Consequently, our time calls for dialogue between various factions of the church for the purpose of better self-understanding and improved relationships. A movement toward the center will ultimately be more true to the spirit of Christianity and more productive in the collective action of the Christian church in this country.

Chapter Twelve

Church vs. Secularism

The major doctrinal difference centrists have with the right and the left is in the area of ecclesiology, the doctrine of the church. Centrists believe it is essential to recognize that the biblical teaching is that the church is the only divine institution within a fallen society. The major mistake of both the Moral Majority and the WCC is in their failure to understand that the church is the primary focus of God's activity in the world.

Biblical Considerations about the Church
The scripture teaches that the church is the one aspect of the social order which is not under the dominion of the powers. The church is a unique "society within the society," having been created by God as his "chosen people, a royal priesthood, a holy nation, a people belonging to God" (I Peter 2:9). What makes the church unique is that it is the only extension of Jesus in the world, the only presence of the future Kingdom, the only manifestation of the New Creation. According to St. Paul the church is in a struggle with the evil powers that rule society. This struggle is "against the rulers, against the authorities, against the powers of this dark world, and against the spiritual forces of evil in the heavenly realm" (Eph. 6:12). Paul warns against

superhuman demonic powers which control the minds, hearts, and actions of a fallen human society and determine the outcome of human events. These are the powers that are at work behind the personal and cultural manifestations of violence, greed, selfishness, immorality, and the general decadence of society.

Consequently, the focus of God's work in the world is in the church, not in a particular nation or in any other group. God has not raised up America or the Marxist revolution to save the world. He only saves the world through Jesus Christ who is manifested in history in the church. Therefore, the true meaning of history is not dependent on a nation, nor will God's Kingdom be brought to the world through moral betterment or social liberation. Rather, the instrument of God's Kingdom, the focus of his activity for the salvation of the world, is the church alone.

Furthermore, the church is the source of Christian values. God has revealed himself and his values to the church especially in the incarnation of his Son who by his life, example, and teaching imaged the way his church is to live. Thus, the revelation of God's values has been given to the church and the church is called to guard, preserve, and pass on these values.

For these reasons the role of the church in a society governed by the powers is to be a prophetic witness. In a sense the church witnesses to the reality of God by its very existence. The presence of the church around the world and throughout history is a clear witness to the existence of a God who loves and cares for his world and is active in it. Furthermore, the church is a witness against the powers. The ultimate power in this world is the power of Christ who in his death and resurrection defeated the powers of death, of evil, and the dominion of the devil. Even though the powers of evil still rage, the church is the continuing witness to the ultimate destruction of the powers in the consummation. The church, as the presence of the future, is a witness against the powers because it alone is free from their control. For this reason the church acts as a social critic. It denounces the powers and their evil effects in society and calls on people who are under the powers to renounce them and turn to Jesus Christ in the life of the church, the society of people whose allegiance is to the victor over the powers.

But how does the church relate to the secular world? How Jesus was present to the world is a clue to the relationship the church must sustain to America today. Jesus was *identified* with the world, he was *separate* from the powers of the world, and he came to *transform* the world by his death and resurrection. These three relationships which Jesus sustained to the world are the general guidelines for the role of the church in today's world.[1] But how? How does the church fulfill these roles in the contemporary American society, given the recognition that America is dominated by the "powers"?

The Church Identifies with the World

First, the church must recognize its *identification* with the American society. By identification, the centrist means two things. First, the people of the church must live out their lives in the context of American culture—secular or not. In this respect Christians are not easily distinguishable from other people. Diognetus, a second-century writer, described Christians this way: "Christians cannot be distinguished from the rest of the human race by country or language or customs. They do not live in cities of their own; they do not use a peculiar form of speech; they do not follow an eccentric manner of life."[2] On the positive side this means that Christians are good citizens: they lead quiet and content lives; they pay their taxes; they pray for their rulers.

Second, the church is identified with society in that it is an institution within society, along with the state and the family. However, it is a unique institution, for it has to do with *the structure of meaning.* It alone witnesses to transcendence, anticipates the consummation, and has received the revelation of true values. For this reason the presence of the church is a witness to the true meaning of the world. Diognetus speaks to this relationship using a Platonic analogy: "What the soul is in the body, that Christians are in the world."[3] Put simply, this means that the church is the heart of the world. The true meaning of the world radiates out from it to the whole of society. For this reason the church is "light" and "salt." It points the way to the truth and makes life more tolerable simply by its existence in the world.

However, there are false and harmful ways for the church to identify with society. In the case of both the right and the left there is an "over-identification" with the goals of society which borders on civil religion. Civil religion implies that the church seeks to fulfill its goals through the power structures of the government. In the case of the Moral Majority their unabashed identification with "American foundations" and the "free enterprise system" identifies them with a particular social outlook and program. The same can be said for the World Council of Churches. Their identification with "socialism," "the Marxist critique," and the "liberation movements" gives them a particular identification as well. The problem with such ironclad party commitment is that the hope of the church in society is shifted from the action of the church to the work of the party. It places the *focus* of God's activity in the world in a political structure rather than in the church, God's people in society.

Centrists believe, therefore, that it is imperative for the institutional church to remain bipartisan. This means that the institutional church must never organize as a political bloc or a power structure. The purpose of the church is to worship, to evangelize, and to live out the life of Christ as prophet and priest. The church as an institution must speak out on issues, but to organize as a political power is a denial of its true character, a compromise of its essential purpose and place in the world. For in this the hope of the church is shifted from the consummation to the state, a structure which is governed by the powers.

On the other hand, it is legitimate for individual Christians to organize members of the Christian community to be a witness against the evils of the state or some other evil aspect of the social order. However, the temptation these groups must avoid is the love of power which leads to control and the utopian hope of achieving kingdom values within a societal structure not committed to Jesus Christ. The danger is twofold. First, Christian groups by legislating morality may fool themselves into thinking they have created a Christian nation (no such thing is possible). Second, to insure the perpetuation of their "Christian nation" they may be tempted to rule in a totalitarian way denying the relationship between order and freedom. So long as Christians remember that they are confronting fallen power structures which cannot be converted, their work will be meaningful in the knowledge that they are acting as a witness to Christ's work and inviting others into Jesus Christ and his church, the only hope of the world.

The Church Is Separated from the Powers

The second relationship of the church to society is *separational*. Centrists understand this term to refer to the separation of the church from the ideologies that rule the world. Paul frequently speaks of these ideologies and calls people to "put off" a commitment to these powers and to be "renewed in the spirit of your minds, and put on the new nature, created after the likeness of God in true righteousness and holiness" (Eph. 4:23-24).

But how do we flesh out this antithesis? Consider the following three suggestions.

First, the most crucial witness to the "church in antithesis" to the prevailing culture must take place in the corporate lifestyle of the church. The church is a "society within society" and as such is characterized by a set of values which is distinctly over against the values of society.

For example, secular humanism has made a god of materialism resulting in the cult of consumerism; it has made a god of sensualism resulting in the cult of sexual permissiveness; it has made a god of "self-interest" resulting in the cult of narcissism. These conditions can be illustrated by the clothes we wear, the cars we drive, the vacations we take, the foods we eat, the houses we live in, and the day to day decisions we make out of the secular values which run our life. The church as God's community of people on earth is called to live by a different set of values.

The church as the corporate body of Christ is called to live out of self-giving, moral restraint, and concern for others. If there is any point at which the church in America has truly failed, it has been her inability to express a "corporate otherness." For the most part the church's corporate life has become secularized by the values of American culture. The desire for success, power, wealth, and position by Christians has drastically reduced the impact which the church could make in America. Political power, legislative influence, and the cloud of lobbyists will never proximate the power of an alternative Christian lifestyle.

The second-century epistle of Diognetus describes the antithesis of the church to culture in these words:

They dwell in their own countries, but simply as sojourners. As citizens, they share in all things as if foreigners. Every foreign land is to them as their native country, and every land of their birth as land of strangers. They marry, as do all others; they beget children; but they do not destroy their offspring. They have a common table, but not a common bed. They are in the flesh but they do not live after the flesh. They pass their days on earth, but they are citizens of heaven. They obey the prescribed laws, and at

. the same time surpass the laws by their lives. They love all men, and are persecuted by all. They are unknown and condemned; they are put to death, and restored to life. They are poor, yet make many rich; they are in lack of all things, and yet abound in all; they are dishonoured, and yet in their very dishonour are glorified. They are evil spoken of, and yet are justified; they are reviled, and bless; they are insulted, and repay the insult with honour; they do good, yet are punished as evil-doers. When punished, they rejoice as if quickened into life; they are assailed by the Jews as foreigners, and are persecuted by the Greeks; yet those who hate them are unable to assign any reason for their hatred.[4]

Second, the antithesis of the church to the American culture must be expressed through a confrontation with the powers. For this reason centrists approve of the "moral issue" concerns of the Moral Majority and insist that Christians must *practice* Christian morality by leading exemplary lives. Christians must be honest in their business dealings, moral in their relationships, stable in their families, resistant to alcoholism and drugs, nonpatronizing to television programs and movies which promote sexual permissiveness. On the other hand centrists agree with the issues on the left. Christians are to serve the people of the world, feed the hungry, clothe the poor, and free the oppressed. But these works of charity are done by the church through the agencies of the church. The church must not become dependent on the nation as God's tool of righteousness because the primary focus of God's work in the world is in the church. Therefore, the church must visibly and corporately express its lifestyle as one of antithesis to the ways of the world in order that it may have the resources and the freedom to be "salt" and "light," the vehicle through which God is working in the world as a demonstration of his power and as an example of those values which characterize his kingdom.

Both the right and the left have a sense of this confrontation. The Moral Majority points to the immoral decadence of a corrupt society. The left points to oppression, injustice, and discrimination. The centrist believes both issues are of great importance because they deal with the control of the alien powers over the minds, hearts, and souls of people. So long as these "powers" are in control of people, they will be reflected in the culture which people unfold. This is the case in America. The reliance on self and the affirmation of a world devoid of any ultimate point of reference has had a disastrous effect on the whole of culture and the values by which people live. The church as the people of God is called to stand against these forces and engage in battle with them in the power of Christ.

Furthermore, this battle is not in the abstract. It takes place in concrete situations with those who control education, television, and advertising. It is found in the courts where legislation is made, and in the voting booth where we elect persons of understanding and power. It is a battle which opposes materialism, sensualism, greed, injustice, and oppression of every kind wherever it is found.

Sometimes the confrontation of the powers takes the form of a counterculture movement as it did in monasticism, a movement of protest against the growing worldliness of the church. In our age there are a number of signs of a Christian countercultural movement. It is not only taking shape in the emerging communities, but in the Christian school movement, television, unions, lobby movements, publishing houses, retirement centers, and vacation areas.

Centrists are not against the creation of a Christian counterculture and recognize the need and value of these movements in the face of growing secularism. Nevertheless, the centrist cautions against an abandonment of a witness within existing structures for fear they may no longer contain a witness against the powers. Furthermore, centrists fear an underlying antiintellectualism and subsequent lack of quality in the current counterculture movement. Unfortunately, most counterculture Christian movements display these very weaknesses.

Third, the notion of the church as a community of antithesis contains some very important implications for Christian vocation. First, it suggests that Christians cannot do any kind of work indiscriminately. This viewpoint is illustrated in the pre-Constantinian church. *The Apostolic Tradition* of Hippolytus makes it clear that people who wanted to become part of the church had to quit jobs that compromised Christian commitment. A Christian was not allowed to be an idol maker, a charioteer in the shows, a soldier of war, or an astrologer, among others. Today we shrink from the thought that a Christian could run a pornographic theater, perform abortions, or kill in guerrilla warfare.

Second, while some occupations are strictly forbidden for the Christian, others must be scrutinized very carefully because of the compromise of Christian values they demand. Involvement in a business whose sole purpose is profit, or acceptance of a position in an international company known to discriminate, to dehumanize, to pollute the air and water, and to contribute to economic inequalities are highly questionable. The Christian is not free to have one set of ethics at home and another at work. One must bring the Christian ethic to work and function with as much consistency as possible, realizing that at some point one may have to confront the company and refuse to carry out its orders because of the compromise involved.

The Church Is a Transforming Presence

The third model of the church in America relating to society is *transformational*. That is, Christians are called to be a transforming presence in society, to function in every legitimate area of life in such a way that Christ may be transfigured in relationships, in the work of our hands, in the products of our mind, in society itself.

The notion of transformation is rooted in the death, resurrection, and consummation of Christ. In his death, "He disarmed the principalities and powers and made a public example of them, triumphing over them in him" (Col. 2:15). In his resurrection he demonstrated the possibilities of a new creation. Paul puts it this way: "Therefore, if any one is in Christ, he is a new creation, the old has passed away, behold the new has come" (2 Cor. 5:17). In the consummation the "powers" of evil which have not yet been put down will be totally destroyed (Rev. 20) and God will create a "new heaven and a new earth" (Rev. 21).

The Christian church functions out of this perspective. It knows that evil has been defeated at the cross and will be ultimately and finally destroyed in the consummation. Therefore, the church is called to live now in resurrection power as the new creation, as the presence of the future in society.

How can the church do this in America? To begin with it must be recognized that the church will not usher in the Kingdom. That is God's prerogative alone. Thus, centrists reject all utopian, ideological approaches as a means of transforming society. Nevertheless, because the church is called to be a witness, centrists recognize the need to mediate Christian values into a non-Christian society. Here are four suggestions on how that may be accomplished.

First, centrists believe in the priority of personal evangelism. The church must call people to turn away from the powers and toward a full acceptance of Jesus Christ as Lord. In her witness the church is constantly calling on people to forsake the powers of darkness and come into the light of the gospel. Centrists believe in conversion and the necessity of regeneration as a prerequisite to membership in the body of Christ, the society of people in which God is at work in the world.

Second, centrists call for a transformation of the mind. Conversion affects the whole person including the intellect. The loss of a Christian world view is the work of the enemies of the cross. The minds of American people are caught in the grip of secular humanism which offers no ultimate solution to the problems of humanity and has, as is apparent, yielded confusion and chaos in this country. Although no utopian hope for the conversion of all minds to Jesus Christ ought to be advanced, the words of Charles Malik, the former President of the United Nations, are pertinent. He writes, "No civilization can endure with its mind being as confused and disordered as ours is today. All our ills stem proximately from the false philosophies that have been let loose in the world and that are now being taught in the universities."[5] Therefore, Christians must enter the arena of politics, economics, psychology, science, philosophy, the arts and sciences, and all other academic disciplines as witnesses to the Christian world view, bringing the gospel to bear on the mind and inviting the intelligentsia to enter into the domain of Christ and his church.

Third, centrists must press the claims of Christ and his rule in every area of the social order. The church needs to make its voice more prominent in societal matters, speaking the prophetic word, confronting the government and other aspects of the social order with the claims of Christ and his church. But it must be remembered that this confrontation is a witness, not an attempt to take over the social order and make it obey the moral mandates of the Christian faith. That would be moralism. The claim of the church goes deeper. It calls people to regeneration and invites them to enter the church, where true values are lived out. Through the witness of the church the immorality of society may be temporarily restrained. But to hope to convert the powers and to create a Christian nation or society is to reject Christian eschatology. Only God can do that and only after the consummation when the powers of evil have been completely destroyed.

Finally, there is a vocational implication to the notion of transformation. It is this: Christians should seek servant roles within society in order to mediate Christ's love in a personal way within the structures dominated by evil. For example, vocations which are sometimes pursued for prestige, power, or money may be turned into vocations of service: a medical doctor or nurse may give his or her talent to serving the poor; a lawyer may establish a legal aid society to assist the poor and minorities; a teacher may seek to question the powers and raise doubts about their ultimacy; a social worker may mediate compassion and love in assisting those in need to find purpose in life and meaningful work; a counselor may serve the needy without the demands of a high price. These works of love can be done, not only by individuals, but by parachurch organizations. There is a continuing need for crisis pregnancy centers, orphanages, retirement centers, and food and clothing outlets for the needy. Many centrists are already engaged in these vocations and many more are needed as the vision of Christian service to the social order becomes a priority for Christian people.

Conclusion
It has been argued that the role of the church in American society is worked out in the tensions which exist between identification, separation, and transformation. In conclusion, some specific applications of these stances to the Moral Majority and the World Council of Churches need to be made.

First, centrists call on the right and the left to adopt a biblical position of identification. Specifically, centrists challenge the right and the left to abandon partisan politics, to recognize that God is not on the side of free enterprise or republicanism, nor is he on the side of socialism or the democratic ticket. God is on the side of the church. It is through the church and its ministry to the world that God is working out his purpose of salvation.

Therefore, centrists call on all the churches, left, right, middle, to recognize the need for each local church *to be* the church in the world. That is, Christians must recognize that their attitudes, actions, and lifestyle are to be modeled after Christ, that they are his body in the world, an extension of himself. Thus, the church is an "alien" and a "sojourner" in the world. Its ultimate hope is not in the kingdoms and power of this world, but in Christ and his kingdom.

Nevertheless, the church carries a great responsibility to this world because Christ continues his redemptive work through the church in the world. For this reason there is a triumphant note in the voice of the church. Christ's defeat of sin at the cross, his demonstration of power over death in the resurrection, and the promise of a new creation at his coming again assure the church of victory over evil, both personal and social. Therefore, centrists call upon the right and the left to renew the battle with both personal and social evil. Centrists call upon the Moral Majority to expand their moral concerns to include an attack against those structures of economic and social injustice which create conditions of poverty, hunger, and discrimination. Centrists also call upon the World Council of Churches and their American National affiliate to rise up to protect personal moral standards and to confront those institutions which are guilty of eroding Christian values in our society. But this must be done in the name and power of Christ and his church and not in the name of a particular economic and political system. We all must learn to trust God to work in and through the prophetic voice and action of his church.

Chapter Thirteen

The Future

Reference has already been made to the major issues facing the world today. The staggering number and complexity of these issues confuses many people. They don't know how to get a handle on the overwhelming difficulty of today's problems.

Nevertheless, it may be argued that this confusing array of issues may be grouped together under four basic problems which beg for Christian responsibility. These problems are like trees having a trunk with many branches. In this chapter we will examine the trunk, so to speak, from which all the branches stem. By clarifying the issues Christians will be able to see where the prophetic voice of the church should be spoken and obtain some vision of a Christian vocation in one or more of these areas. These four "trunks" are the sanctity of human life, the order of existence, the stewardship of creation, and moral order.

The Sanctity of Human Life
One of the foundational teachings of the Christian world view is the conviction that human life is sacred. This viewpoint is derived from the Genesis account that human beings are made in the image of God (Genesis 1:26) and from the dust of the ground (Genesis 2:7). These two

phrases speak to the paradox of human existence. Persons belong to the ground, they are of the earth, of the natural order of things. Yet, persons have a *transcendent quality*, they are fearfully and wonderfully made in the image and after the likeness of a personal and infinite God.

This sacred character of human life is reaffirmed and sealed in the doctrine of the incarnation. Scripture teaches that God himself became a man. The "Word," St. John tells us, "became flesh and lived for a while among us" (John 1:14). St. Paul sees Jesus as "the image of the invisible God" (Col. 1:15), and the writer of Hebrews describes Jesus Christ as "the radiance of God's glory and exact representation of his being" (Hebrews 1:3). Thus, the scripture affirms that people are sacred not only because they are made in the image of God, but also because God imaged himself in a real person, Jesus Christ.

The fact that God became a man and lived his life out in the various stages of human existence was treated by the early church as an expression of the sanctification of every stage of life. For example, Irenaeus, a second-century theologian, wrote, "he sanctified every stage of life by a likeness to himself. He came to save all through his own person; all, that is, who through him are re-born to God; infants, children, boys, young men and old. Therefore, he passed through every stage of life."[1]

Consequently, centrists believe that the sanctity of human life as taught in the scripture and affirmed by the church applies to a number of issues facing the American society. Centrists insist that the notion that human persons are sacred must be applied equally to the issues of abortion, euthanasia, the destruction of humanity by a nuclear war, the moral issues raised by genetic manipulation, and the problem of the quality of human life as it pertains to the poor and oppressed of the world.

For example, centrists believe it is a contradiction to take up the cause of the right to life of the fetus and ignore the issue of nuclear war or vice versa.

An excellent example of the centrist position on the sanctity of human life is found in the following *Pastoral Letter to the Episcopal Church* written and sent to the local churches by the Bishops of Tennessee (October 2-9, 1980):

Since we hold that human life is sacred, our political choices need to reflect the best judgment we can make as to the people and platforms that honor all persons—that respond to the needs of the aged, the unemployed, and the disadvantaged—that uphold racial and sexual equality—and that resist irresponsible and indiscriminate abortion as a heedless, casual birth control option.

Our political choices also need to reflect a moral resolve that American economic structures reduce the extremities of arrogant wealth and gross poverty which mark doomed societies. Callous biblical kingdoms were brought low by God's wrath. Contemporary societies are likewise under judgment for greed and indifference to human need. "What do you mean by crushing my people, by grinding the face of the poor? says the Lord God of hosts" (Isaiah 3:15).

A further imperative that flows from the sacredness of human life is Christ's call that his disciples be peacemakers. Wherever possible, our voting needs to call to account the iniquity of a runaway arms capability that supplies small nations with lethal weaponry, much of it American. Our political action must deplore the daily and deadly addition that America makes to the absurd stockpile of nuclear warheads. We now have atomic megatons adequate to kill everybody in the Soviet Union twenty times over.

Since nuclear armaments here and in the Soviet Union have created a world in which the whole can nowhere be protected against its parts, our own national security has reached the zero point. The issue is no longer the survival of one nation against another. We stand now in mortal danger of global human incineration. A computer error could trigger mutually assured destruction. American responsibility for the world beyond us compels a moral outcry against the arms race.

The Order of Existence
A second underlying assumption of scripture is the convic-

tion that creation is characterized by order. Creation is not chaotic, nor lacking in meaning. God, who is himself an ordered being, has stamped the image of order on his own creation. For example, Christian theology recognizes order within the Godhead between Father, Son, and Holy Spirit. This is not, as some would argue, a fixed hierarchical order, but a dynamic relational quality within the Godhead. Likewise a centrist view of order in the creation (which bears the stamp of the Creator) is not hierarchical, but relational.

Centrists recognize the natural order of creation. There is a movement of time from moment to moment, year to year and season to season. Likewise there is an order between various social groupings. For example, a basic distinction is made between the family, the church, and the state. Even within these social units there is an ordering of relationships. In the family, distinctions are made between the function of husband, wife, and children. In the church distinctions are made between bishops, ministers, deacons, and the laity with their variety of gifts. In the state distinctions are made between the various offices and the citizenry. Not every culture orders its relationships in the same way. But all cultures do have an ordering of relationships.[2]

An important feature of the ordering of society is the issue of the *relationship* between the family, the church, and the state. This is an extremely important issue today. To what extent may the government control the church or the family? The underlying issue is the ordering of relationships. The centrists appreciate the work done in this area by the Reformers and especially the thought of the Reformed philosophers like Abraham Kuyper and Herman Dooyeeweerd.

They argue for a sphere sovereignty for each societal unit, yet recognize that the dynamic nature of life and society demand that the issue of interrelatedness between societal units must be a matter of continual discussion resulting in a delicate and reasoned balance. The need for careful thought and action is made more clear when one realizes that totalitarianism results when one sphere rules absolutely over the other. In America today the danger of totalitarianism comes from the elevation of the government to a position of authority over the family, the church, education, business, and other institutions. In this matter centrists agree with the concern of the Moral Majority. For example, consider some of the issues that face the courts today:

1. Can religious student groups constitutionally meet like other student groups on public college and university campuses?
2. Can a church fire a homosexual staff member in the face of a local gay rights ordinance prohibiting the same?
3. Can home Bible studies be prevented by zoning ordinances requiring that only churches can be used for such purposes?
4. Are the chaplaincy programs in the armed services and in our many jails and prisons an unconstitutional "establishment of religion"?
5. Is the teaching in the public schools of humanistic values, including sex education courses and others which are clearly antagonistic to traditional Judeo-Christian values, an unconstitutional establishment of religion?
6. Can religiously-affiliated adoption and foster care agencies employ religious criteria in the selection of homes for children?
7. To what extent can religious individuals and groups be limited in their efforts to influence the political process?
8. What regulations of private Christian schools—both secondary schools and institutions of higher education—are proper, and which are excessive?
9. What limitations can constitutionally be placed on our access to public places (auditoriums and schools, as well as quasi-public places such as commercial areas) for evangelistic or other religious purposes?
10. What should the respective roles of the state and parents be in the raising of children? (Such questions arise, for example, in

the distribution of contraceptives or performing abortions to and on minors without notice or consent, challenges of parents' rights to use corporal punishment, etc.)[3]

The threat to the creational balance between the state, the church, and the family comes from human sinfulness. Sin finds expression in a power group that will do anything to achieve its ends. When a power group autonomously determines what is right or wrong and seeks to exercise its power over the other spheres, totalitarianism results.

For example, when the government decides it has the power in and of itself to define human values, determine the content of material taught in education, redefine the family, or impose controls on the church, then that government has overstepped its bounds and is acting in a totalitarian way.

Totalitarianism is a matter of concern in America because that is the trend of the American government. An example is the following recommendation of the White House Family Conference: "Delegates . . . agreed on the vital need for family-life education, and that government at all levels should assist the public and private sectors by providing appropriate courses for children and parents." The point is this: Who gives the government the right to define and propagate views concerning the family? The government is not the source of values. The government does not have a revelation from God saying what is right and/or wrong. The attempt to define a family as any two people who live together (as has been suggested) will result in government sanction of homosexual marriages.

The question of government interference in the family is only one of many issues. The government has been spreading its power into all the institutions of life, including the church. The consequence of government control in all areas of life will be the ruination of pluralism, a major factor in the American experiment.

This issue points up the necessity of the church as a mediating structure. Because the church is the primary source of values, it must be free to continue to transmit these values to society by means of its free and uninhibited witness. The church must resist government decisions that contradict Christian values. In this way Christians will resist the temptation to place a near-Messianic trust in the nation and will find a renewed source of power in their commitment to Jesus Christ and his ultimate lordship over all of life.

But there is another side of the coin as well: the church must not control the government. The church is the extension of Jesus Christ in the world. The government is an organization within fallen society that has its origin in the fallen nature of things. Thus, the role of the church in the world and the role of the government in the world are two completely different things.

According to Romans 13, God has appointed government within the fallen creation to be "God's servant, an agent of wrath to bring punishment on the wrongdoers." Consequently, government has the responsibility to restrain evil, to make rules and regulations to hold evil in check, and to punish the wrongdoer. In this sense the Christian is to "submit himself to the governing authorities" because they have been "established by God" and "hold no terror for those who do right." But these statements suggest a fairly limited view of government. No Christian is to give ultimate allegiance to an earthly government. At best a Christian allegiance to government is only conditional. When a government oversteps its bounds and demands an action or a subscription to a value which contradicts what the Christian knows to be true by the revelation given to the church, the Christian is free to disobey through a form of nonviolent resistance (see Acts 4:19-20).

Fortunately, we live in a democratic society where we have the freedom to criticize the government, to vote, to lobby for change and make an impact on the formation of government and its ways of governing the people.

Christians ought not to back away from this responsibility and calling. The civil rights movement, the protest of the war in Viet Nam, and now the demand for morality in government officials and legislation are all valuable forms of Christian witness. It is exceedingly important, however, that this witness be bipartisan, lest a branch of the church gain political control. If the church gains control, we can expect a Christian totalitarianism which is no less desirable than a non-Christian totalitarianism. The church must remain a witness to the truth and mediate its perspective without gaining control. Only in this way can the delicate balance between freedom and order in society be maintained.

The Stewardship of Creation
Another group of contemporary issues cluster around the Christian conviction that we are called to be stewards of creation. This notion of stewardship must be understood in the context of the biblical assertion that God is the owner of all things.

The Old Testament repeatedly asserts God's ownership over creation in phrases like "all the earth is mine" (Ex. 19:5) or in declarations like that of David that "the earth is the Lord's and everything in it, the world, and all who live in it" (Ps. 24:1). In the New Testament Paul speaks of the relationship between Christ and creation reminding his readers that "all things were created by him and for him" and that "in him all things hold together" (Col. 1:16-17). Therefore, a starting point for the Christian view of stewardship is that everything is God's—all of the earth, its riches, its treasures, and resources belong to him. In this context there are two clear statements God makes regarding the relationship between persons and nature. First, humans have been given a position of dominion in the creation, and second they are called to the task of servanthood within the creation.[4]

First, the position of dominion is derived from the command of God in Genesis 1:26, "Let them rule" and Genesis 1:28, "fill the earth and subdue it." From these verses the Christian church has recognized the "cultural mandate" which places human persons over the creation.

However, there is another side to the relationship which human persons have with nature. They are a part of it. In Genesis 2 God, we are told, "formed man from the dust of the ground." This view of human persons, together with the assertion that humans are to have "dominion," states a paradox of human existence: human beings are called to have dominion over nature of which they are a part. Thus, the Bible speaks to the delicate relationship between human persons and the rest of the creation suggesting that it is abnormal for the human part of creation to be at variance with the non-human creation.

However, because of the fall and subsequent development of human sinfulness, an abnormal enmity developed between humans and the rest of creation. Consequently, humans perverted the meaning of dominion and, instead of living in harmony with nature, abused nature and its resources for their own selfish ends. Consequently, the exploitation of nature and its resources is not a result of Christian teaching as some have asserted, but the result of the sinful condition of human beings expressed in personal and national greed—the plundering of natural resources for personal comfort and luxury. This exploitive approach to nature has resulted in our current ecological imbalance, the pollution of our air and water, the raping of land, and military contest for the security of oil and mineral rights.

It is for this reason Christians must remember that the Bible teaches also the corollary responsibility that dominion implies: the task of servanthood in creation. Genesis 2:15 tells us that God "took the man and put him in the Garden of Eden to work it and take care of it." The implication is that human beings have been given the responsibility of the management of creation.

It must be kept in mind that this management extends to the whole of creation for the needs of all. We must be concerned about that part of nature which is "common to all." No single person or group can claim total rights over such necessities as air, water, food, and fuel which are needed for the basic necessities of human existence. Consequently, nations, corporations, and individual people must be held accountable for the use, misuse, and abuse of these common elements. The current ecological and energy crises are two examples of major concern for the whole world.

These issues also bear on the responsibility the rich have toward the poor, not only personally, but in a national and global sense. It is simply wrong for one-third of the world to consume a large portion of the world's resources and food, while the other two-thirds of the world lives in need.

The church's role as steward of creation arises from the biblical teaching about man in relation to nature as exemplified in Jesus Christ. In his incarnation he became part of human existence, by his example he displayed a concern for the needy, in his death and resurrection he conquered sin so that those who are united to him by faith may be free from an exploitive enmity toward creation. Because the church knows these values, it is called to mediate them into the world today. There are several ways in which the church may accomplish this goal.

First, the church must witness against the narcissistic self-interest of our age which leads people into the mad scramble for personal wealth, the pursuit of luxuries, and the desire to accumulate the latest gadgets. Second, the church must press the vocation of service in the area of environment and energy as a servant occupation for Christians. Third, the church must make Christians and people in general aware of those political decisions which will fall on the side of environmental support and more equal distribution of the world's wealth. But the church must do this as a witness through proclamation, nonviolent resistance, and voting without becoming partisan, thus avoiding entanglement with the political process.

Moral Order

A fourth area of general concern is that of personal and community morals. One of the most pervasive problems of contemporary culture is the decline of morality in every facet of American life and the rise of permissiveness. The Moral Majority has effectively pointed up the loss of moral standards in the family, education, television, and the contemporary arts.

In the face of moral decadence the church must not remain silent. But *how* are we to speak to these questions is the issue. In order to focus on that question, we must ask first what is the basis of moral order and second what implications does this understanding hold for the life of the church in the world today?

The question of the basis of the moral order is too large to be fully covered in this book. Nevertheless an outline answer may be seen in the following four points.

First, the origin of morality is found in revelation. As William Barclay says, "Ethics . . . is not what convention tells me to do, but what God commands me to do."[5] The point is, that whatever humankind knows about right and wrong does not come from trial and error, nor custom, but from "thus saith the Lord." The supreme example of this approach to morality is found in the giving of the Ten Commandments to Israel.

Second, the roots of morality are found in history. God has a right to speak because he is the Creator and Lord of history. Consequently, the history of the Old Testament shows us that God chose a people to whom he spoke the word of morality. They were a historical people who entered into a covenant relationship with God, accepted Yahweh as their God and agreed to the moral terms of the covenant. They were his unique people, called to live their lives out in obedience to his will articulated in the moral terms of the covenant. In many ways the history of Israel is a history of their failure to keep the covenant.

Third, the example of morality is found in Jesus Christ, God Incarnate. He lived in history in absolute obedience to the moral commands which he himself as God had given by revelation to Israel. Thus, Jesus is the living embodiment of revealed morality, expressed in a historical place and time. For this reason the witness to Jesus' life—his moral concerns, his relationship with people, his example as recorded in scripture—is the ultimate point of reference for Christian ethics. For this reason Paul could write to the Galatians that they should "fulfill the law of Christ" (6:2).

Fourth, the locus of morality today must therefore be in the church. The church as the extension of Jesus in the world is to live out the example and teachings of Jesus. The church is Jesus to the world. The church is the only visible and tangible form of Jesus which is available to the world. It is the community of his body and therefore the very presence of the Lord of history in history.

These four basic principles concerning the basis of morality hold several implications for the church today.

First, the church advocates regeneration, not moralism. Moralism is do-goodism, a self-motivated morality which could be achieved apart from regeneration. What the church calls for is a renewal of character through regeneration into Jesus Christ and the community of his people. In the body of his people, the individual grows into a moral consciousness with the whole community which is living in collective obedience to the will of God.

Second, this understanding of morality is both an indictment and a challenge to the contemporary church. The church is not yet what it should be. In some places it promotes values which are distinctly pagan; in other places it has so accommodated itself to worldly power and success that it has become reprobate. Therefore, the American church must repent, turn away from its worldliness, and seek to be renewed in its own morals under the Lordship of Christ, by the power of the Holy Spirit.

Third, Christians must become more aware of personal and public moral issues as they relate to their own commitment in the church. We cannot practice a double ethic—one in the church and another in the world. We must be willing to take the risk of applying the ethic of Jesus in whatever vocational calling we pursue.

Conclusion

These four issues—the sanctity of human life, the order of existence, the stewardship of creation, and moral order—speak to the entire range of ethical issues which confront our world today. They are, of course, issues with which both the Moral Majority and the World Council of Churches are concerned. The difference, so far as the prophetic center is concerned, between these groups is not as much with the issues as with the ideology that stands behind them. The error of both the Moral Majority and the World Council of Churches is that they place too much trust in an earthly economic and political system as the structure through which they deal with these problems.

The prophetic center differs with the right and left because it approaches these problems through a Christ-centered view of the church. The church, as the extended presence of Jesus Christ in the world, is both the source of values and the only hope of the world. The solution to the world's problems does not lie in an economic or political system, nor does it lie in the predominance of America. It lies only in Jesus Christ who, through the church, speaks his word to the world.

The hope of the church and the ultimate allegiance of Christians is, therefore, to Christ and his Kingdom only— and the present visible concrete witness to and instrument of his Kingdom is the church. In and through the church we mediate the values of the Kingdom to the world. This is our calling, our witness to the world. And while we believe temporary change is possible and that here and there Christian values will be adopted in society, we have no utopian hopes to establish the Kingdom on earth apart from the consummation of Christ's work in his second coming.

I should like to conclude with an invitation to the Moral Majority and the World Council of Churches to forsake their economic and political alignments and to return to a Christocentric understanding of the church as the presence of Jesus in the world. If the centrist's interpretation of the church in the world is scriptural, there is no adequate reason why we cannot hope for the day we will work together in witness to the Kingdom.

Appendixes:

Recent Centrist Documents

1. The Chicago Declaration 1973
2. The Lausanne Covenant 1974
3. The Chicago Call 1977
4. An Evangelical Commitment to Simple Lifestyle 1980

Appendix One

The Chicago Declaration

In November of 1973 more than fifty evangelical leaders met at the YMCA building in Chicago to draft a call to evangelicals to return to active social involvement. The coordinator of that event was Ron Sider.

As evangelical Christians committed to the Lord Jesus Christ and the full authority of the Word of God, we affirm that God lays total claim upon the lives of His people. We cannot, therefore, separate our lives in Christ from the situation in which God has placed us in the United States and the world.

We confess that we have not acknowledged the complete claims of God on our lives.

We acknowledge that God requires love. But we have not demonstrated the love of God to those suffering social abuses.

We acknowledge that God requires justice. But we have not proclaimed or demonstrated His justice to an unjust American society. Although the Lord calls us to defend the social and economic rights of the poor and the oppressed, we have mostly remained silent. We deplore the historic involvement of the church in America with racism, and the conspicuous responsibility of the evangelical community for perpetuating the personal attitudes and institutional structures that have divided the body of Christ along color lines. Further, we have failed to condemn the exploitation of racism at home and abroad by our economic system.

We affirm that God abounds in mercy and that He forgives all who repent and turn from their sins. So we call our fellow evangelical Christians to demonstrate repentance in a Christian discipleship that confronts the social and political injustice of our nation.

We must attack the materialism of our culture and the maldistribution of the nation's wealth and services. We recognize that as a nation we play a crucial role in the imbalance and injustice of international trade and development. Before God and a billion hungry neighbors, we must rethink our values regarding our present standard of living and promote more just acquisition and distribution of the world's resources.

We acknowledge our Christian responsibilities of citizenship. Therefore, we must challenge the misplaced trust of the nation in economic and military might—a proud trust that promotes a national pathology of war and violence which victimizes our neighbors at home and abroad. We must resist the temptation to make the nation and its institutions objects of near-religious loyalty.

We acknowledge that we have encouraged men to prideful domination and women to irresponsible passivity. So we call both men and women to mutual submission and active discipleship.

We proclaim no new gospel, but the Gospel of our Lord Jesus Christ, who, through the power of the Holy Spirit, frees people from sin so that they might praise God through works of righteousness.

By this declaration, we endorse no political ideology or party, but call our nation's leaders and people to that righteousness which exalts a nation.

We make this declaration in the Biblical hope that Christ is coming to consummate the Kingdom, and we accept His claim on our total discipleship till He comes.

The Lausanne Covenant

In July of 1974 the International Congress on World Evangelization met for the purpose of theological study and the development of an international strategy for evangelism. This gathering was sponsored by the World Evangelical Fellowship. *The Lausanne Covenant,* which was largely the work of Angelican clergyman John R. W. Stott and his committee, was approved by the participants representing more than 150 nations.

Introduction
We, members of the Church of Jesus Christ, from more than 150 nations, participants in the International Congress on World Evangelization at Lausanne, praise God for his great salvation and rejoice in the fellowship he has given us with himself and with each other. We are deeply stirred by what God is doing in our day, moved to penitence by our failures and challenged by the unfinished task of evangelization. We believe the Gospel is God's good news for the whole world, and we are determined by his grace to obey Christ's commission to proclaim it to all mankind and to make disciples of every nation. We desire, therefore, to affirm our faith and our resolve, and to make public our covenant.

1. The Purpose of God
   We affirm our belief in the one eternal God, Creator and Lord of the world, Father, Son and Holy Spirit, who governs all things according to the purpose of his will. He has been calling out from the world a people for himself, and sending his people back into the world to be his servants

and his witnesses, for the extension of his kingdom, the building up of Christ's body, and the glory of his name. We confess with shame that we have often denied our calling and failed in our mission, by becoming conformed to the world or by withdrawing from it. Yet we rejoice that even when borne by earthen vessels the Gospel is still a precious treasure. To the task of making that treasure known in the power of the Holy Spirit we desire to dedicate ourselves anew.

(Isa. 40:28; Matt. 28:19; Eph. 1:11; Acts 15:14; John 17:6, 18; Eph. 4:12; I Cor. 5:10; Rom. 12:2; II Cor. 4:7)

2. *The Authority and Power of the Bible*

We affirm the divine inspiration, truthfulness and authority of both Old and New Testament Scriptures in their entirety as the only written Word of God, without error in all that it affirms, and the only infallible rule of faith and practice. We also affirm the power of God's Word to accomplish his purpose of salvation. The message of the Bible is addressed to all mankind. For God's revelation in Christ and in Scripture is unchangeable. Through it the Holy Spirit still speaks today. He illumines the minds of God's people in every culture to perceive its truth freshly through their own eyes and thus discloses to the whole church ever more of the many-colored wisdom of God.

(II Tim. 3:16; II Pet. 1:21; John 10:35; Isa. 55:11; I Cor. 1:21; Rom. 1:16; Matt. 5:17,18; Jude 3; Eph. 1:17,18; 3:10,18)

3. *The Uniqueness and Universality of Christ*

We affirm that there is only one Savior and only one Gospel, although there is a wide diversity of evangelistic approaches. We recognize that all men have some knowledge of God through his general revelation in nature. But we deny that this can save, for men suppress the truth by their unrighteousness. We also reject as derogatory to Christ and the Gospel every kind of syncretism and dialogue which implies that Christ speaks equally through all religions and ideologies. Jesus Christ, being himself the only God-man, who gave himself as the only ransom for sinners, is the only mediator between God and man. There is no other name by which we must be saved. All men are perishing because of sin, but God loves all men, not wishing that any should perish but that all should repent. Yet those who reject Christ repudiate the joy of salvation and condemn themselves to eternal separation from God. To proclaim Jesus as "the Savior of the world" is not to affirm that all men are either automatically or ultimately saved, still less to affirm that all religions offer salvation in Christ. Rather it is to proclaim God's love for a world of sinners and to invite all men to respond to him as Savior and Lord in the wholehearted personal commitment of repentance and faith. Jesus Christ has been exalted above every other name; we long for the day

when every knee shall bow to him and every tongue shall confess him
Lord.

(Gal. 1:6-9; Rom. 1:18-32; I Tim. 2:5,6; Acts 4:12; John 3:16-19; II Pet. 3:9;
II Thess. 1:7-9; John 4:42; Matt. 11:28; Eph. 1:20,21; Phil. 2:9-11)

4. The Nature of Evangelism

To evangelize is to spread the good news that Jesus Christ died for our
sins and was raised from the dead according to the Scriptures, and that as
the reigning Lord he now offers the forgiveness of sins and the liberating
gift of the Spirit to all who repent and believe. Our Christian presence in
the world is indispensable to evangelism, and so is that kind of dialogue
whose purpose is to listen sensitively in order to understand. But evangelism itself is the proclamation of the historical biblical Christ as Savior
and Lord, with a view to persuading people to come to him personally
and so be reconciled to God. In issuing the Gospel invitation we have no
liberty to conceal the cost of discipleship. Jesus still calls all who would
follow him to deny themselves, take up their cross, and identify themselves with his new community. The results of evangelism include
obedience to Christ, incorporation into his church and responsible service in the world.

(I Cor. 15:3,4; Acts 2:32-39; John 20:21; I Cor. 1:23; II Cor. 4:5;
5:11,20; Luke 14:25-33; Mark 8:34; Acts 2:40,47; Mark 10:43-45)

5. Christian Social Responsibility

We affirm that God is both the Creator and the Judge of all men. We
therefore should share his concern for justice and reconciliation throughout human society and for the liberation of men from every kind of
oppression. Because mankind is made in the image of God, every person, regardless of race, religion, color, culture, class, sex or age, has an
intrinsic dignity because of which he should be respected and served, not
exploited. Here too we express penitence both for our neglect and for
having sometimes regarded evangelism and social concern as mutually
exclusive. Although reconciliation with man is not reconciliation with
God, nor is social action evangelism, nor is political liberation salvation,
nevertheless we affirm that evangelism and socio-political involvement
are both part of our Christian duty. For both are necessary expressions of
our doctrines of God and man, our love for our neighbor and our obedience to Jesus Christ. The message of salvation implies also a message of
judgment upon every form of alienation, oppression and discrimination,
and we should not be afraid to denounce evil and injustice wherever they
exist. When people receive Christ they are born again into his kingdom
and must seek not only to exhibit but also to spread its righteousness in
the midst of an unrighteous world. The salvation we claim should be
transforming us in the totality of our personal and social responsibilities.
Faith without works is dead.

(Acts 17:26,31; Gen. 18:25; Isa. 1:17; Psa. 45:7; Gen. 1:26,27;
Jas. 3:9; Lev. 19:18; Luke 6:27,35; Jas. 2:14-26; John 3:3,5;
Matt. 5:20; 6:33; II Cor. 3:18; Jas. 2:20)

6. The Church and Evangelism

We affirm that Christ sends his redeemed people into the world as the
Father sent him, and that this calls for a similar deep and costly penetra-
tion of the world. We need to break out of our ecclesiastical ghettos and
permeate non-Christian society. In the church's mission of sacrificial
service evangelism is primary. World evangelization requires the whole
church to take the whole Gospel to the whole world. The church is at the
very center of God's cosmic purpose and is his appointed means of
spreading the Gospel. But a church which preaches the Cross must itself
be marked by the Cross. It becomes a stumbling block to evangelism
when it betrays the Gospel or lacks a living faith in God, a genuine love
for people, or scrupulous honesty in all things including promotion and
finance. The church is the community of God's people rather than an
institution, and must not be identified with any particular culture, social
or political system, or human ideology.

(John 17:18; 20:21; Matt. 28:19,20; Acts 1:8; 20:27; Eph. 1:9,10;
3:9-11; Gal. 6:14,17; II Cor. 6:3,4; II Tim. 2:19-21; Phil. 1:27)

7. Cooperation in Evangelism

We affirm that the church's visible unity in truth is God's purpose.
Evangelism also summons us to unity, because our oneness strengthens
our witness, just as our disunity undermines our gospel of reconciliation.
We recognize, however, that organizational unity may take many forms
and does not necessarily forward evangelism. Yet we who share the
same biblical faith should be closely united in fellowship, work and
witness. We confess that our testimony has sometimes been marred by
sinful individualism and needless duplication. We pledge ourselves to
seek a deeper unity in truth, worship, holiness and mission. We urge the
development of regional and functional cooperation for the furtherance
of the church's mission, for strategic planning, for mutual encouragement, and for the sharing of resources and experience.

(John 17:21,23; Eph. 4:3,4; John 13:35; Phil. 1:27; John 17:11-23)

8. Churches in Evangelistic Partnership

We rejoice that a new missionary era has dawned. The dominant role
of western missions is fast disappearing. God is raising up from the
younger churches a great new resource for world evangelization, and is
thus demonstrating that the responsibility to evangelize belongs to the
whole body of Christ. All churches should therefore be asking God and
themselves what they should be doing both to reach their own area and

to send missionaries to other parts of the world. A re-evaluation of our missionary responsibility and role should be continuous. Thus a growing partnership of churches will develop and the universal character of Christ's Church will be more clearly exhibited. We also thank God for agencies which labor in Bible translation, theological education, the mass media, Christian literature, evangelism, missions, church renewal, and other specialist fields. They too should engage in constant self-examination to evaluate their effectiveness as part of the Church's mission.

(Rom. 1:8; Phil. 1:5; 4:15; Acts 13:1-3; I Thess. 1:6-8)

9. The Urgency of the Evangelistic Task

More than 2,700 million people, which is more than two-thirds of mankind, have yet to be evangelized. We are ashamed that so many have been neglected; it is a standing rebuke to us and to the whole church. There is now, however, in many parts of the world an unprecedented receptivity to the Lord Jesus Christ. We are convinced that this is the time for churches and para-church agencies to pray earnestly for the salvation of the unreached and to launch new efforts to achieve world evangelization. A reduction of foreign missionaries and money in an evangelized country may sometimes be necessary to facilitate the national church's growth in self-reliance and to release resources for unevangelized areas. Missionaries should flow ever more freely from and to all six continents in a spirit of humble service. The goal should be, by all available means and at the earliest possible time, that every person will have the opportunity to hear, understand, and receive the good news. We cannot hope to attain this goal without sacrifice. All of us are shocked by the poverty of millions and disturbed by the injustices which cause it. Those of us who live in affluent circumstances accept our duty to develop a simple life-style in order to contribute more generously to both relief and evangelism.

(John 9:4; Matt. 9:35-38; Rom. 9:1-3; I Cor. 9:19-23; Mark 16:15; Isa. 58:6,7; Jas. 1:27; 2:1-9; Matt. 25:31-46; Acts 2:44,45; 4:34,35)

10. Evangelism and Culture

The development of strategies for world evangelization calls for imaginative pioneering methods. Under God, the result will be the rise of churches deeply rooted in Christ and closely related to their culture. Culture must always be tested and judged by Scripture. Because man is God's creature, some of his culture is rich in beauty and goodness. Because he has fallen, all of it is tainted with sin and some of it is demonic. The Gospel does not presuppose the superiority of any culture to another, but evaluates all cultures according to its own criteria of truth and righteousness, and insists on moral absolutes in every culture. Missions have all too frequently exported with the Gospel an alien culture, and churches have sometimes been in bondage   culture rather than to the Scripture. Christ's evangelists must humbly seek to empty themselves of all but their personal authenticity in order to become the servants of others, and churches must seek to transform and enrich culture, all for the glory of God.

(Mark 7:8,9,13; Gen. 4:21,22; I Cor. 9:19-23; Phil. 2:5-7; II Cor. 4:5)

11. Education and Leadership

We confess that we have sometimes pursued church growth at the expense of church depth, and divorced evangelism from Christian nurture. We also acknowledge that some of our missions have been too slow to equip and encourage national leaders to assume their rightful responsibilities. Yet we are committed to indigenous principles, and long that every church will have national leaders who manifest a Christian style of leadership in terms not of domination but of service. We recognize that there is a great need to improve theolological education, especially for church leaders. In every nation and culture there should be an effective training program for pastors and laymen in doctrine, discipleship, evangelism, nurture and service. Such training programs should not rely on any stereotyped methodology but should be developed by creative local initiatives according to biblical standards.

(Col. 1:27,28; Acts 14:23; Tit. 1:5,9; Mark 10:42-45; Eph. 4:11,12)

12. Spiritual Conflict

We believe that we are engaged in constant spiritual warfare with the principalities and powers of evil, who are seeking to overthrow the church and frustrate its task of world evangelization. We know our need to equip ourselves with God's armor and to fight this battle with the spiritual weapons of truth and prayer. For we detect the activity of our enemy, not only in false ideologies outside the church, but also inside it in false gospels which twist Scripture and put man in the place of God. We need both watchfulness and discernment to safeguard the biblical Gospel. We acknowledge that we ourselves are not immune to worldliness of thought and action, that is, to a surrender to secularism. For example, although careful studies of church growth, both numerical and spiritual, are right and valuable, we have sometimes neglected them. At other times, desirous to insure a response to the Gospel, we have compromised our message, manipulated our hearers through pressure techniques, and become unduly preoccupied with statistics or even dishonest in our use of them. All this is worldly. The church must be in the world; the world must not be in the church.

(Eph. 6:12; II Cor. 4:3,4; Eph. 6:11,13-18; II Cor. 10:3-5;
I John 2:18-26, 4:1-3; Gal. 1:6-9; II Cor. 2:17, 4:2; John 17:15)

13. Freedom and Persecution

It is the God-appointed duty of every government to secure conditions of peace, justice, and liberty in which the church may obey God, serve the Lord Christ, and preach the Gospel without interference. We, therefore, pray for the leaders of the nations and call upon them to guarantee freedom of thought and conscience, and freedom to practice and propagate religion in accordance with the will of God and as set forth in The Universal Declaration of Human Rights. We also express our deep concern for all who have been unjustly imprisoned, and especially for our brethren who are suffering for their testimony to the Lord Jesus. We promise to pray and work for their freedom. At the same time we refuse to.be intimidated by their fate. God helping us, we too will seek to stand against injustice and to remain faithful to the Gospel, whatever the cost. We do not forget the warnings of Jesus that persecution is inevitable.

(I Tim. 1:1-4; Acts 4:19, 5:29; Col. 3:24; Heb. 13:1-3; Luke 4:18; Gal. 5:11, 6:12; Matt. 5:10-12; John 15:18-21)

14. The Power of The Holy Spirit

We believe in the power of the Holy Spirit. The Father sent his Spirit to bear witness to his Son; without his witness ours is futile. Conviction of sin, faith in Christ, new birth, and Christian growth are all his work. Further, the Holy Spirit is a missionary spirit; thus evangelism should arise spontaneously from a Spirit-filled church. A church that is not a missionary church is contradicting itself and quenching the Spirit. Worldwide evangelization will become a realistic possibility only when the Spirit renews the church in truth and wisdom, faith, holiness, love, and power. We, therefore, call upon all Christians to pray for such a visitation of the sovereign Spirit of God that all his fruit may appear in all his people and that all his gifts may enrich the body of Christ. Only then will the whole church become a fit instrument in his hands, that the whole earth may hear his voice.

(I Cor. 2:4; John 15:26,27, 16:8-11; I Cor. 12:3; John 3:6-8; II Cor. 3:18; John 7:37-39; I Thess. 5:19; Acts 1:8; Psa. 85:4-7; 67:1-3; Gal. 5:22,23; I Cor. 12:4-31; Rom. 12:3-8)

15. The Return of Christ

We believe that Jesus Christ will return personally and visibly, in power and glory, to consummate his salvation and his judgment. This promise of his coming is a further spur to our evangelism, for we remember his words that the Gospel must first be preached to all nations. We believe that the interim period between Christ's ascension and return is to be filled with the mission of the people of God, who have no liberty to stop before the end. We also remember his warning that false Christs and false prophets will arise as precursors of the final Antichrist. We, therefore, reject as a proud, self-confident dream the notion that man can ever build a utopia on earth. Our Christian confidence is that God will perfect his kingdom, and we look forward with eager anticipation to that day, and to the new heaven and earth in which righteousness will dwell and God will reign forever. Meanwhile, we rededicate ourselves to the service of Christ and of men in joyful submission to his authority over the whole of our lives.

(Mark 14:62; Heb. 9:28; Mark 13:10; Acts 1:8-11; Matt. 28:20; Mark 13:21-23; John 2:18, 4:1-3; Luke 12:32; Rev. 21:1-5; II Pet. 3:13; Matt. 28:18)

Conclusion

Therefore, in the light of this our faith and our resolve, we enter into a solemn covenant with God and with each other, to pray, to plan, and to work together for the evangelization of the whole world. We call upon others to join us. May God help us by his grace and for his glory to be faithful to this our covenant! Amen, Alleluia!

Appendix 3

The Chicago Call

In May of 1977 a group of forty-five evangelicals representing a cross section of Protestant denominations as well as
Catholic Evangelicals gathered near Chicago to issue a call
to evangelicalism. The essential feature of the statement
issued on that occasion was to call evangelicals back to
historic Christianity. The document is being included here
because it is evidence of the broader range of issues which
are becoming increasingly important to the evangelical centrists. The chairperson was Robert Webber.

Prologue
  In every age the Holy Spirit calls the church to examine its faithfulness
to God's revelation in Scripture. We recognize with gratitude God's
blessing through the evangelical resurgence in the church. Yet at such a
time of growth we need to be especially sensitive to our weaknesses. We
believe that today evangelicals are hindered from achieving full maturity
by a reduction of the historic faith. There is, therefore, a pressing need to
reflect upon the substance of the biblical and historic faith and to recover
the fullness of this heritage. Without presuming to address all our needs,
we have identified eight of the themes to which we as evangelical Christians must give careful theological consideration.

A Call to Historic Roots and Continuity
  We confess that we have often lost the fullness of our Christian heritage, too readily assuming that the Scriptures and the Spirit make us
independent of the past. In so doing, we have become theologically

shallow, spiritually weak, blind to the work of God in others and married to our cultures.

Therefore we call for a recovery of our full Christian heritage. Throughout the church's history there has existed an evangelical impulse to proclaim the saving, unmerited grace of Christ, and to reform the church according to the Scriptures. This impulse appears in the doctrines of the ecumenical councils, the piety of the early fathers, the Augustinian theology of grace, the zeal of the monastic reformers, the devotion of the practical mystics and the scholarly integrity of the Christian humanists. It flowers in the biblical fidelity of the Protestant Reformers and the ethical earnestness of the Radical Reformation. It continues in the efforts of the Puritans and Pietists to complete and perfect the Reformation. It is reaffirmed in the awakening movements of the 18th and 19th centuries which joined Lutheran, Reformed, Wesleyan and other evangelicals in an ecumenical effort to renew the church and to extend its mission in the proclamation and social demonstration of the Gospel. It is present at every point in the history of Christianity where the Gospel has come to expression through the operation of the Holy Spirit: in some of the strivings toward renewal in Eastern Orthodoxy and Roman Catholicism and in biblical insights in forms of Protestantism differing from our own. We dare not move beyond the biblical limits of the Gospel; but we cannot be fully evangelical without recognizing our need to learn from other times and movements concerning the whole meaning of that Gospel.

A Call to Biblical Fidelity

We deplore our tendency toward individualistic interpretation of Scripture. This undercuts the objective character of biblical truth, and denies the guidance of the Holy Spirit among his people through the ages.

Therefore we affirm that the Bible is to be interpreted in keeping with the best insights of historical and literary study, under the guidance of the Holy Spirit, with respect for the historic understanding of the church.

We affirm that the Scriptures, as the infallible Word of God, are the basis of authority in the church. We acknowledge that God uses the Scriptures to judge and to purify his Body. The church, illumined and guided by the Holy Spirit, must in every age interpret, proclaim and live out the Scriptures.

A Call to Creedal Identity

We deplore two opposite excesses: a creedal church that merely recites a faith inherited from the past, and a creedless church that languishes in a doctrinal vacuum. We confess that as evangelicals we are not immune from these defects.

Therefore we affirm the need in our time for a confessing church that will boldly witness to its faith before the world, even under threat of persecution. In every age the church must state its faith over against heresy and paganism. What is needed is a vibrant confession that excludes as well as includes, and thereby aims to purify faith and practice. Confessional authority is limited by and derived from the authority of Scripture, which alone remains ultimately and permanently normative. Nevertheless, as the common insight of those who have been illumined by the Holy Spirit and seek to be the voice of the "holy catholic church," a confession should serve as a guide for the interpretation of Scripture.

We affirm the abiding value of the great ecumenical creeds and the Reformation confessions. Since such statements are historically and culturally conditioned, however, the church today needs to express its faith afresh, without defecting from the truths apprehended in the past. We need to articulate our witness against the idolatries and false ideologies of our day.

A Call to Holistic Salvation

We deplore the tendency of evangelicals to understand salvation solely as an individual, spiritual and otherworldly matter to the neglect of the corporate, physical and this-worldly implication of God's saving activity.

Therefore we urge evangelicals to recapture a holistic view of salvation. The witness of Scripture is that because of sin our relationships with God, ourselves, others and creation are broken. Through the atoning work of Christ on the cross, healing is possible for these broken relationships.

Wherever the church has been faithful to its calling, it has proclaimed personal salvation; it has been a channel of God's healing to those in physical and emotional need; it has sought justice for the oppressed and disinherited; and it has been a good steward of the natural world.

As evangelicals we acknowledge our frequent failure to reflect this holistic view of salvation. We therefore call the church to participate fully in God's saving activity through work and prayer, and to strive for justice and liberation for the oppressed, looking forward to the culmination of salvation in the new heaven and new earth to come.

A Call to Sacramental Integrity

We decry the poverty of sacramental understanding among evangelicals. This is largely due to the loss of our continuity with the teaching of many of the Fathers and Reformers and results in the deterioration of sacramental life in our churches. Also, the failure to appreciate the sacramental nature of God's activity in the world often leads us to disregard the sacredness of daily living.

Therefore we call evangelicals to awaken to the sacramental implications of creation and incarnation. For in these doctrines the historic church has affirmed that God's activity is manifested in a material way. We need to recognize that the grace of God is mediated through faith by the operation of the Holy Spirit in a notable way in the sacraments of baptism and the Lord's Supper. Here the church proclaims, celebrates and participates in the death and resurrection of Christ in such a way as to nourish her members throughout their lives in anticipation of the consummation of the kingdom. Also, we should remember our biblical designation as "living epistles," for here the sacramental character of the Christian's daily life is expressed.

A Call to Spirituality

We suffer from a neglect of authentic spirituality on the one hand, and an excess of undisciplined spirituality on the other hand. We have too often pursued a superhuman religiosity rather than the biblical model of a true humanity released from bondage to sin and renewed by the Holy Spirit.

Therefore we call for a spirituality which grasps by faith the full content of Christ's redemptive work: freedom from the guilt and power of sin, and newness of life through the indwelling and outpouring of his Spirit. We affirm the centrality of the preaching of the Word of God as a primary means by which his Spirit works to renew the church in its corporate life as well as in the individual lives of believers. A true spirituality will call for identification with the suffering of the world as well as the cultivation of personal piety.

We need to rediscover the devotional resources of the whole church, including the evangelical traditions of Pietism and Puritanism. We call for an exploration of devotional practice in all traditions within the church in order to deepen our relationship both with Christ and with other Christians. Among these resources are such spiritual disciplines as prayer, meditation, silence, fasting, Bible study and spiritual diaries.

A Call to Church Authority

We deplore our disobedience to the Lordship of Christ as expressed through authority in his church. This has promoted a spirit of autonomy in persons and groups resulting in isolationism and competitiveness, even anarchy, within the body of Christ. We regret that in the absence of godly authority, there have arisen legalistic, domineering leaders on the one hand and indifference to church discipline on the other.

Therefore we affirm that all Christians are to be in practical submission to one another and to designated leaders in a church under the Lordship of Christ. The church, as the people of God, is called to be the visible presence of Christ in the world. Every Christian is called to active priesthood in worship and service through exercising spiritual gifts and ministries. In the church we are in vital union both with Christ and with one another. This calls for community with deep involvement and mutual commitment of time, energy and possessions. Further, church discipline, biblically based and under the direction of the Holy Spirit, is essential to the well-being and ministry of God's people. Moreover, we encourage all Christian organizations to conduct their activities with genuine accountability to the whole church.

A Call to Church Unity

We deplore the scandalous isolation and separation of Christians from one another. We believe such division is contrary to Christ's explicit desire for unity among his people and impedes the witness of the church in the world. Evangelicalism is too frequently characterized by an ahistorical, sectarian mentality. We fail to appropriate the catholicity of historic Christianity, as well as the breadth of the biblical revelation.

Therefore we call evangelicals to return to the ecumenical concern of the Reformers and the later movements of evangelical renewal. We must humbly and critically scrutinize our respective traditions, renounce sacred shibboleths, and recognize that God works within diverse historical streams. We must resist efforts promoting church union-at-any-cost, but we must also avoid mere spiritualized concepts of church unity. We are convinced that unity in Christ requires visible and concrete expressions. In this belief, we welcome the development of encounter and cooperation within Christ's church. While we seek to avoid doctrinal indifferentism and a false irenicism, we encourage evangelicals to cultivate increased discussion and cooperation, both within and without their respective traditions, earnestly seeking common areas of agreement and understanding.

An Evangelical Commitment to Simple Lifestyle

This document was written and endorsed by the International Consultation on Simple Lifestyle, held at Hoddesdon, England on March 17-21, 1980. The Consultation was sponsored by the World Evangelical Fellowship Theological Commission's Unit on Ethics and Society (Dr. Ronald Sider, Chairman) and the Lausanne Committee on World Evangelization's Lausanne Theology and Education Group (John Stott, Chairman).

For four days we have been together, 85 Christians from 27 countries, to consider the resolve expressed in the Lausanne Covenant (1974) to "develop a simple lifestyle." We have tried to listen to the voice of God, through the pages of the Bible, through the cries of the hungry poor, and through each other. And we believe God has spoken to us.

We thank God for his great salvation through Jesus Christ, for his revelation in Scripture which is a light for our path, and for the Holy Spirit's power to make us witnesses and servants in the world.

We are disturbed by the injustice of the world, concerned for its victims, and moved to repentance for our complicity in it. We have also been stirred to fresh resolves, which we express in this Commitment. March 1980

1. Creation
We worship God as the Creator of all things, and we celebrate the goodness of his creation. In his generosity he has given us everything to enjoy, and we receive it from his hands with humble thanksgiving

(I Timothy 4:4, 6:17). God's creation is marked by rich abundance and diversity, and he intends its resources to be husbanded and shared for the benefit of all.

We therefore denounce environmental destruction, wastefulness and hoarding. We deplore the misery of the poor who suffer as a result of these evils. We also disagree with the drabness of the ascetic. For all these deny the Creator's goodness and reflect the tragedy of the fall. We recognize our own involvement in them, and we repent.

2. Stewardship

When God made man, male and female, in his own image, he gave them dominion over the earth (Genesis 1:26-28). He made them stewards of its resources, and they became responsible to him as Creator, to the earth which they were to develop, and to their fellow human beings with whom they were to share its riches. So fundamental are these truths that authentic human fulfillment depends on a right relationship to God, neighbor and the earth with all its resources. People's humanity is diminished if they have no just share in those resources.

By unfaithful stewardship, in which we fail to conserve the earth's finite resources, to develop them fully, or to distribute them justly, we both disobey God and alienate people from his purpose for them. We are determined, therefore, to honor God as the owner of all things, to remember that we are stewards and not proprietors of any land or property that we may have, to use them in the service of others, and to seek justice with the poor who are exploited and powerless to defend themselves.

We look forward to "the restoration of all things" at Christ's return (Acts 3:21). At that time our full humanness will be restored; so we must promote human dignity today.

3. Poverty and Wealth

We affirm that involuntary poverty is an offense against the goodness of God. It is related in the Bible to powerlessness, for the poor cannot protect themselves. God's call to rulers is to use their power to defend the poor, not to exploit them. The church must stand with God and the poor against injustice, suffer with them and call on rulers to fulfill their God-appointed role.

We have struggled to open our minds and hearts to the uncomfortable words of Jesus about wealth. "Beware of covetousness" he said, and "a person's life does not consist in the abundance of his possessions" (Luke 12:15). We have listened to his warnings about the danger of riches. For wealth brings worry, vanity and false security, the oppression of the weak and indifference to the sufferings of the needy. So it is hard for a rich person to enter the kingdom of heaven (Matthew 19:23), and the greedy will be excluded from it. The kingdom is a free gift offered to all, but it is especially good news for the poor because they benefit most from the changes it brings.

We believe that Jesus still calls some people (perhaps even us) to follow him in a lifestyle of total, voluntary poverty. He calls all his followers to an inner freedom from the seduction of riches (for it is impossible to serve God and money) and to sacrificial generosity ("to be rich in good works, to be generous and ready to share"—1 Timothy 6:18). Indeed, the motivation and model for Christian generosity are nothing less than the example of Jesus Christ himself, who, though rich, became poor that through his poverty we might become rich (2 Corinthians 8:9). It was a costly, purposeful self-sacrifice; we mean to seek his grace to follow him. We resolve to get to know poor and oppressed people, to learn issues of injustice from them, to seek to relieve their suffering, and to include them regularly in our prayers.

4. The New Community

We rejoice that the church is the new community of the new age, whose members enjoy a new life and a new lifestyle. The earliest Christian church, constituted in Jerusalem on the Day of Pentecost, was characterized by a quality of fellowship unknown before. Those Spirit-filled believers loved one another to such an extent that they sold and shared their possessions. Although their selling and giving were voluntary, and some private property was retained (Acts 5:4), it was made subservient to the needs of the community. "None of them said that anything he had was his own" (Acts 4:32). That is, they were free from the selfish assertion of proprietary rights. And as a result of their transformed economic relationships, "there was not a needy person among them" (Acts 4:34).

This principle of generous and sacrificial sharing, expressed in holding ourselves and our goods available for people in need, is an indispensable characteristic of every Spirit-filled church. So those of us who are affluent in any part of the world, are determined to do more to relieve the needs of less privileged believers. Otherwise, we shall be like those rich Christians in Corinth who ate and drank too much while their poor brothers and sisters were left hungry, and we shall deserve the stinging rebuke Paul gave them for despising God's church and desecrating Christ's body (1 Corinthians 11:20-24). Instead, we determine to resemble them at a later stage when Paul urged them out of their abundance to give to the impoverished Christians of Judea "that there may be equality" (2 Corinthians 8:10-15). It was a beautiful demonstration of caring love and of Gentile-Jewish solidarity in Christ.

In this same spirit, we must seek ways to transact the church's corporate business together with minimum expenditure on travel, food and accommodation. We call on churches and para-church agencies in their planning to be acutely aware of the need for integrity in corporate life-style and witness.

Christ calls us to be the world's salt and light, in order to hinder its social decay and illumine its darkness. But our light must shine and our salt must retain its saltness. It is when the new community is most obviously distinct from the world—in its values, standards and life-style—that it presents the world with a radically attractive alternative and so exercises its greatest influence for Christ. We commit ourselves to pray and work for the renewal of our churches.

5. Personal Lifestyle

Jesus our Lord summons us to holiness, humility, simplicity and contentment. He also promises us his rest. We confess, however, that we have often allowed unholy desires to disturb our inner tranquility. So without the constant renewal of Christ's peace in our hearts, our emphasis on simple living will be one-sided.

Our Christian obedience demands a simple lifestyle, irrespective of the needs of others. Nevertheless, the facts that 800 million people are destitute and that about 10,000 die of starvation every day make any other lifestyle indefensible.

While some of us have been called to live among the poor, and others to open our homes to the needy, all of us are determined to develop a simpler lifestyle. We intend to reexamine our income and expenditure, in order to manage on less and give away more. We lay down no rules or regulations, for either ourselves or others. Yet we resolve to renounce waste and oppose extravagance in personal living, clothing and housing, travel and church buildings. We also accept the distinction between necessities and luxuries, creative hobbies and empty status symbols, modesty and vanity, occasional celebrations and normal routine, and between the service of God and slavery to fashion. Where to draw the line requires conscientious thought and decision by us, together with members of our family. Those of us who belong to the West need the help of our Third World brothers and sisters in evaluating our standards of spending. Those of us who live in the Third World acknowledge that we too are exposed to the temptation to covetousness. So we need each other's understanding, encouragement and prayers.

6. International Development

We echo the words of the Lausanne Covenant: "We are shocked by the poverty of millions, and disturbed by the injustices which cause it." One quarter of the world's population enjoys unparalleled prosperity, while another quarter endures grinding poverty. This gross disparity is an intolerable injustice; we refuse to acquiesce in it. The call for a New

International Economic Order expresses the justified frustration of the Third World.

We have come to understand more clearly the connection between resources, income and consumption: people often starve because they cannot afford to buy food, because they have no income, because they have no opportunity to produce, and because they have no access to power. We therefore applaud the growing emphasis of Christian agencies on development rather than aid. For the transfer of personnel and appropriate technology can enable people to make good use of their own resources, while at the same time respecting their dignity. We resolve to contribute more generously to human development projects. Where people's lives are at stake, there should never be a shortage of funds.

But the action of governments is essential. Those of us who live in the affluent nations are ashamed that our governments have mostly failed to meet their targets for official development assistance, to maintain emergency food stocks or to liberalize their trade policies.

We have come to believe that in many cases multi-national corporations reduce local initiative in the countries where they work, and tend to oppose any fundamental change in government. We are convinced that they should become more subject to controls and more accountable.

7. Justice and Politics

We are also convinced that the present situation of social injustice is so abhorrent to God that a large measure of change is necessary. Not that we believe in an earthly utopia. But neither are we pessimists. Change can come, although not through commitment to simple lifestyle or human development projects alone.

Poverty and excessive wealth, militarism and the arms industry, and the unjust distribution of capital, land and resources are issues of power and powerlessness. Without a shift of power through structural change these problems cannot be solved.

The Christian church, along with the rest of society, is inevitably involved in politics which is "the art of living in community." Servants of Christ must express his lordship in their political, social and economic commitments and their love for their neighbors by taking part in the political process. How, then, can we contribute to change?

First, we will pray for peace and justice, as God commands. Second, we will seek to educate Christian people in the moral and political issues involved, and so clarify their vision and raise their expectations. Third, we will take action. Some Christians are called to special tasks in government, economics or development. All Christians must participate in the active struggle to create a just and responsible society. In some situations obedience to God demands resistance to an unjust established order. Fourth, we must be ready to suffer. As followers of Jesus, the Suffering Servant, we know that service always involves suffering.

While personal commitment to change our lifestyle without political action to change systems of injustice lacks effectiveness, political action without personal commitment lacks integrity.

8. Evangelism

We are deeply concerned for the vast millions of unevangelized people in the world. Nothing that has been said about lifestyle or justice diminishes the urgency of developing evangelistic strategies appropriate to different cultural environments. We must not cease to proclaim Christ as Saviour and Lord throughout the world. The church is not yet taking seriously its commission to be his witnesses "to the ends of the earth" (Acts 1:8).

So the call to a responsible lifestyle must not be divorced from the call to responsible witness. For the credibility of our message is seriously diminished whenever we contradict it by our lives. It is impossible with integrity to proclaim Christ's salvation if he has evidently not saved us from greed, or his lordship if we are not good stewards of our possessions, or his love if we close our hearts against the needy. When Christians care for each other and for the deprived, Jesus Christ becomes more visibly attractive.

In contrast to this, the affluent lifestyle of some Western evangelists when they visit the Third World is understandably offensive to many.

We believe that simple living by Christians generally would release considerable resources of finance and personnel for evangelism as well as development. So by our commitment to a simple lifestyle we recommit ourselves wholeheartedly to world evangelization.

9. The Lord's Return

The Old Testament prophets both denounced the idolatries and injustices of God's people and warned of his coming judgment. Similar denunciations and warnings are found in the New Testament. The Lord Jesus is coming back soon to judge, to save and to reign. His judgment will fall upon the greedy (who are idolaters) and upon all oppressors. For on that day the King will sit upon his throne and separate the saved from the lost. Those who have ministered to him by ministering to one of the least of his needy brothers and sisters will be saved, for the reality of saving faith is exhibited in serving love. But those who are persistently indifferent to the plight of the needy, and so to Christ in them, will be irretrievably lost (Matthew 25:31-46). All of us need to hear again this solemn warning of Jesus, and resolve afresh to serve him in the deprived. We therefore call on our fellow Christians everywhere to do the same.

Our Resolve

So then, having been freed by the sacrifice of our Lord Jesus Christ, in obedience to his call, in heartfelt compassion for the poor, in concern for evangelism, development and justice, and in solemn anticipation of the Day of Judgment, we humbly commit ourselves to develop a just and simple lifestyle, to support one another in it and to encourage others to join us in this commitment.

We know that we shall need time to work out its implications and that the task will not be easy. May Almighty God give us his grace to be faithful! Amen.

Notes

Chapter 1: Introduction
[1](New York: Doubleday, 1980).
[2]See David M. Paton (ed.), *Breaking Barriers: Nairobi 1975* (Grand Rapids: Eerdmans, 1976)

Chapter 2: Capitalism
[1]*Listen America* (New York: Doubleday, 1980), pp. 19-20.
[2]Ibid., p. 15.
[3]Ibid., p. 16.
[4]Ibid., p. 20.
[5]Ibid., p. 16.
[6]Ibid
[7]Ibid   p. 18.
[8]Ibid., p. 13.
[9]Ibid., p. 39.
[10]Ibid., p. 15.
[11]Ibid., p. 7.

Chapter 3: A Chosen Nation
[1]*Listen America,* p. 29.
[2]Ibid., p. 30.
[3]Ibid., pp. 33-34.
[4]Ibid., pp. 37-38.
[5]Ibid., p. 40.
[6]Ibid., p. 43.
[7]Ibid., p. 44.
[8]Ibid., pp. 53-54.
[9]Ibid., p. 51.

[10]Ibid., p. 11.
[11]Ibid., pp. 245ff.
[12]Ibid., p. 100.
[13](Downers Grove: InterVarsity Press, 1978), p. 21.
[14]"Moral Majority, A Response to Attack on Basic Values of Millions of Americans," *Conservative Digest,* Jan. 1981, Vol. 7, No. 1, p. 28.

Chapter 4: Moralism
[1]*Listen America,* p. 70.
[2]Ibid., p. 12.
[3]Ibid., p. 117.
[4]Ibid., p. 56.
[5]Ibid., p. 25.
[6]Ibid., p. 8.
[7]Ibid., p. 19.
[8]Ibid., p. 206.
[9]Ibid., pp. 206-207.
[10]Ibid., p. 207.
[11]Ibid., p. 211.
[12]Ibid., p. 192.
[13]Ibid., p. 187.
[14]Ibid., p. 190.
[15]Ibid., p. 277.
[16]Ibid., p. 228.
[17]Ibid., p. 121.
[18]Ibid., p. 124.
[19]Ibid., p. 133.
[20]Ibid., p. 137.
[21]Ibid., p. 182.
[22]Ibid., pp. 185-186.
[23]Ibid., p. 201.
[24]Ibid., pp. 198-203.
[25]Ibid., p. 236.
[26](Downers Grove: InterVarsity Press, 1978), pp. 168-173.

Chapter 5: Socialism
[1]See Walter Rauschenbusch, *Christianity and the Social Crisis,* edited by Robert D. Cross (New York: Harper and Row, 1964).
[2]Walter Rauschenbusch, *A Theology for the Social Gospel* (New York: Abingdon Press, 1945), p. 50.
[3](New York: Scribners, 1960), p. 9.
[4]Ibid., p. 12.
[5](Grand Rapids: Eerdmans, 1976), pp. 7-8.
[6]Gustavo Guitierrez, *A Theology of Liberation,* trans. Cardinal Inds, Sr., and John Eagleson (Maryknoll, NY: Orbis, 1973), p. 15.

[7]See Klaus Bockmuehl, *The Challenge of Marxism: A Christian Response* (Downers Grove: InterVarsity Press, 1980).

Chapter 6: Minority Groups
[1]Vine Deloria, Jr., *God Is Red* (New York: Dell Publishing Co., 1973), p. 70.
[2]Ibid., p. 105.
[3]Ibid., p. 130.
[4]Ibid., p. 274.
[5]Ibid.
[6]Ibid., p. 277.
[7]Ibid., p. 281.
[8]Ibid., p. 282.
[9]See John D. Woodbridge, Mark A. Noll, and Nathan O. Hatch, *The Gospel in America* (Grand Rapids: Zondervan, 1979), pp. 231-232.
[10]Sterling Tucker, *Black Reflections on White Power* (Grand Rapids: Eerdmans, 1970).
[11]Quoted by Tucker, ibid., p. 111.
[12]Ibid., p. 110.
[13]Ibid., p. 112.
[14]Ibid., pp. 112-113.
[15]Ibid., p. 115.
[16]Sterling Tucker, *For Blacks Only* (Grand Rapids: Eerdmans, 1971), p. 8.
[17]Mary R. Beard, *America Through Women's Eyes* (New York: Greenwood Press, 1961), p. 9.
[18]William O'Neill, *The Woman Movement: Feminism in the United States and England* (Chicago: Quadrangle, 1969), p. 18.
[19](Grand Rapids: Eerdmans, 1971).
[20](New York: Simon and Schuster, 1979), p. 86
[21](Englewood Cliffs, NJ: Prentice-Hall, 1971), see ch. 3.
[22]*What Women Want: From the Official Report to the President, the Congress, and the People of the United States,* p. 86.
[23]For an evangelical assessment of liberation theology see Harvey Conn, "Theologies of Liberation: An Overview" and "Theologies of Liberation: Toward a Common View" in Stanley N. Gundry and Alan F. Johnson, *Tensions in Contemporary Theology,* revised ed. (Chicago: Moody Press, 1976), pp. 327-436.

Chapter 7: Liberation
[1]See David M. Paton, *Breaking Barriers: Nairobi 1975* (Grand Rapids: Eerdmans, 1976).
[2]Ibid., pp. 102-103.
[3]Ibid., p. 116.
[4]Paul Bock, *In Search of a Responsible Society* (Philadelphia: Westminster, 1974), p. 53.

⁵*Breaking Barriers,* p. 107.
⁶Ibid.
⁷Ibid., pp. 109–110.
⁸Ibid.
⁹Ibid., p. 111.
¹⁰Ibid., p. 112.
¹¹Ibid., p. 125.
¹²Ibid., pp. 126–129.
¹³Ibid.
¹⁴Ibid., p. 130.
¹⁵Ibid.
¹⁶Ibid., p. 133.
¹⁷Ibid., p. 134.
¹⁸Ibid., p. 135.
¹⁹Ibid., p. 140.

Chapter 8: World View
¹For a biblical treatment of these themes see Robert Webber, *The Secular Saint* (Grand Rapids: Zondervan, 1979), ch. 3 and 4; see also Arthur Holmes, *All Truth Is God's Truth* (Grand Rapids: Eerdmans).

Chapter 9: Civil Religion
¹The two major sources for a centrist interpretation of America are John D. Woodbridge, Mark A. Knoll, and Nathan O. Hatch, *The Gospel in America* (Grand Rapids: Zondervan, 1979) and Robert D. Linder and Richard V. Pierard, *Twilight of the Saints* (Downers Grove: InterVarsity Press, 1978).
²*The Gospel in America,* p. 213.
³Ibid., p. 104.
⁴Ibid., pp. 165–166.
⁵Ibid., p. 167.
⁶Ibid., p. 170.
⁷Ibid., p. 171.
⁸Ibid., p. 173.
⁹Ibid., p. 174.
¹⁰Ibid., p. 271.
¹¹Ibid., p. 238.
¹²Ibid., p. 178.
¹³Ibid., p. 31.
¹⁴Ibid., p. 191ff.
¹⁵Ibid., p. 274.
¹⁶Ibid., p. 216.
¹⁷Ibid., p. 217.

Chapter 10: Private and Public Ethics
[1]Footnotes to the quotations from these documents will not be made since the documents are included in their entirety in the appendix.
[2]Francis Schaeffer and Everett Koop, *Whatever Happened to the Human Race?* (New York: Revell, 1979), pp. 21-24.
[3]See Mark Hatfield, "Finding the Energy to Continue," *Christianity Today,* Feb. 8, 1980, Vol. XXIV, No. 3, pp. 20ff.
[4]See Loren Wilkinson, "Global Housekeeping: Lords or Servants?", *Christianity Today,* June 27, 1980, Vol. XXIV, No. 2.

Chapter 11: Differences
[1](New York: Harper and Row, 1960), p. 371.
[2]See E. P. News Service, Oct. 11, 1980, p. 10.
[3]See Mark Hatfield, *Lonely Walk* (Chappaqua: Christian Herald, 1979).
[4]10-8-80.
[5]11-23-80, "The New Anti-Right."

Chapter 12: Church vs. Secularism
[1]These models are worked out in detail in Robert Webber, *The Secular Saint* (Grand Rapids: Zondervan, 1979).
[2]"In Defense of the Faith," in Cyril C. Richardson, *Early Christian Fathers* (Philadelphia: Westminster Press, 1963), p. 216.
[3]Ibid., p. 218.
[4]Ibid., p. 217.
[5]*The Two Tasks* (Westchester, IL: Cornerstone Books, 1980).

Chapter 13: The Future
[1]*Adversus Haereses* Vol. 1. 1-2, see Henry Bettenson, *Early Church Fathers* (New York: Oxford, 1969), p. 80.
[2]See Abraham Kuyper, *Lectures on Calvinism* (Grand Rapids: Eerdmans, 1961), pp. 78ff.
[3]These questions were given to me in a personal note by Carl Horn, director of estate planning at Wheaton College and part-time advisor to the Christian Legal Society.
[4]See Loren Wilkinson (ed.), *Earth Keeping: Christian Stewardship of Natural Resources* (Grand Rapids: Eerdmans, 1980).
[5]*Ethics in a Permissive Society* (New York: Harper and Row, 1971), p. 14.

Select Bibliography

Blamires, Harry. *Where Do We Stand? An Examination of the Christian's Position in the Modern World* (Ann Arbor: Servant Books, 1980).

Blamires, Harry. *The Christian Mind* (London: SPCK, 1966).

Bockmuehl, Klaus. *The Challenge of Marxism: A Christian Response* (Downers Grove: InterVarsity Press, 1980).

Brock, Paul. *In Search of a Responsible Society: The Social Teachings of the World Council of Churches* (Philadelphia: Westminster Press, 1974).

Brown, Robert McAfee. *Theology in a New Key* (Philadelphia: Westminster Press, 1978).

Conn, Harvey. "Theologies of Liberation: An Overview" and "Theologies of Liberation: Toward a Common View" in Stanley N. Gundry and Alan F. Johnson, *Tensions in Contemporary Theology* (Chicago: Moody Press, 1979), ch. 8 and 9.

Deloria, Vine, Jr. *God Is Red* (New York: Delta, 1979).

Dayton, Donald W. *Discovering an Evangelical Heritage* (New York: Harper and Row, 1976).

Eells, Robert and Bartel Nyberg. *Lonely Walk: The Life of Senator Mark Hatfield* (Chappaqua: Christian Herald Books, 1979).

Ellul, Jacques. *The New Demons* (New York: Seabury Press, 1975).

Falwell, Jerry. *Listen America* (New York: Doubleday, 1980).

Ford, George Wolfgang. *History of Christian Ethics: From the New Testament to Augustine Vol. I.* (Minneapolis: Augsburg, 1979).

Gladwin, John. *God's People in God's World: Biblical Motives For Social Involvement* (Downers Grove: InterVarsity Press, 1979).

Grant, Robert M. *Early Christianity and Society* (New York: Harper and Row, 1977).

Helms, Jesse. *When Free Men Shall Stand* (Grand Rapids: Zondervan, 1976).

Holmes, Arthur. *All Truth Is God's Truth* (Grand Rapids: Eerdmans, 1977).

Jackson, Dave. *Coming Together: All Those Communities and What They're Up To* (Minneapolis: Bethany Fellowship, 1978).

Lewis, C. S. *Mere Christianity* (New York: Macmillan, 1960).

Linder, Robert D. and Richard V. Pierard, *Twilight of the Saints: Biblical Christianity and Civil Religion in America* (Downers Grove: InterVarsity Press, 1978).

Malik, Charles. *The Two Tasks* (Westchester, IL: Cornerstone Books, 1980).

Marty, Martin E. *The Pro and Con Book of Religious America* (Waco: Word, 1975).

Mouw, Richard J. *Political Evangelism* (Grand Rapids: Eerdmans, 1973).

Neuhaus, Richard John. *Christian Faith and Public Policy: Thinking and Acting in the Courage of Uncertainty* (Minneapolis: Augsburg, 1977).

Paton, David (ed.). *Breaking Barriers, Nairobi 1975* (Grand Rapids: Eerdmans, 1976).

Perkins, John. *Let Justice Roll Down* (Glendale, CA: G L Publications, 1976).

Robison, James with Jim Cox. *Save America to Save the World* (Wheaton, IL: Tyndale House, 1980).

Schaeffer, Francis A. and C. Everett Koop, M.D. *Whatever Happened to the Human Race?* (Old Tappan: Revell, 1979).

Scott, Waldren. *Bring Forth Justice* (Grand Rapids: Eerdmans, 1980).

Sider, Ronald J. *Rich Christians in an Age of Hunger* (Downers Grove: InterVarsity Press, 1977).

Stringfellow, William. *An Ethic For Christians and Other Aliens in a Strange Land* (Waco: Word, 1973).

Tucker, Sterling. *Black Reflections on White Power* (Grand Rapids: Eerdmans, 1970).

Viguerie, Richard A. *The New Right: We're Ready to Lead* (Falls Church, VA: The Viguerie Co., 1980).

Wallis, Jim. *Agenda For Biblical People* (New York: Harper and Row, 1976).

Walter, J. A. *Sacred Cows: Exploring Contemporary Idolatry* (Grand Rapids: Zondervan, 1979).

Webber, Robert. *The Secular Saint: A Case For Evangelical Social Responsibility* (Grand Rapids: Zondervan, 1979).

Wilkinson, Loren (ed.). *Earth Keeping: Christian Stewardship of Natural Resources* (Grand Rapids: Eerdmans, 1980).

Woodbridge, John D., Mark A. Noll, and Nathan O. Hatch. *The Gospel in America: Themes in the Story of America's Evangelicals* (Grand Rapids: Zondervan, 1979).

Yoder, John Howard. *The Politics of Jesus* (Grand Rapids: Eerdmans, 1972)

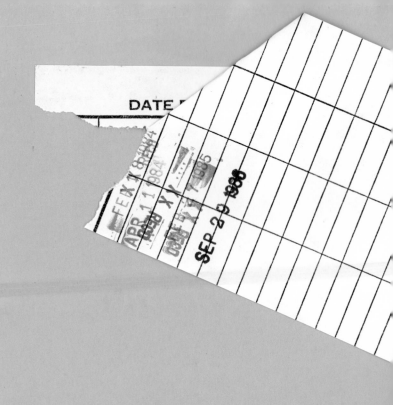